THE LOVE

THE LOVE OF GOD

Martyn Lloyd-Jones

LIFE IN CHRIST □ VOLUME FOUR

STUDIES IN 1 JOHN

CROSSWAY BOOKS

WHEATON, ILLINOIS • NOTTINGHAM, ENGLAND

CREDO

The Love of God

Copyright © 1994 by Elizabeth Catherwood and Ann Desmond.

First U.S. edition published 1994 by Crossway Books, a division of Good News Publishers, 1300 Crescent Street, Wheaton, Illinois 60187

Published in association with Credo Books, P.O. Box 3175, Langley, B.C., Canada V3A 4R5

All rights reserved. No part of this publication may be reproduced, stored in a retrieval system or transmitted in any form by any means, electronic, mechanical, photocopy, recording or otherwise, without the prior permission of the publisher, except as provided by USA copyright law.

Cover illustration: Keith Stubblefield

First printing, 1994

Printed in the United States of America

Library of Congress Cataloging-in-Publication Data
Lloyd-Jones, David Martyn.
   Life in Christ.
   Includes bibliographical references.
   Contents: v. 1. Fellowship with God—v. 2. Walking with God—[etc.]—v. 4. The love of God
   1. Bible. N.T. Epistle of John, 1st—Sermons.   2. Sermons, English.   I. Title.
BS2805.4.L58   1993   227'.9406   92-21507
ISBN 0-89107-814-2

02	01	00	99	98	97	96	95	94
15	14	13	12	11	10	9	8	7	6	5	4	3	2	1

First British Edition 1994

All rights reserved

No part of this publication may be reproduced or transmitted in any form or by any means, electronic, or mechanical, including photocopy, recording or any information storage and retrieval system, without permission in writing from the publisher.

ISBN 1 85684 089-1

Production and Printing in the United States of America for
CROSSWAY BOOKS
Norton Street, Nottingham, England NG7 3HR

TABLE OF CONTENTS

	Acknowledgements	vii
	Note to Readers	ix
1	Test the Spirits	11
2	The All-sufficiency of Christ	25
3	Born of God	37
4	The Manifest Love of God	49
5	We Ought Also . . .	63
6	God Dwells in Us	75
7	The Gift of God's Spirit	91
8	The Fullness of Blessing	103
9	The Apostolic Witness and Testimony	117
10	The Saviour	131
11	Knowing the Love of God	143
12	Dwelling in Love	155
13	That Great Day	167
14	Free from Fear	179
15	Members of the Same Family	193
	Notes	207

ACKNOWLEDGEMENTS

As with previous books in this series, the editing work on these sermons has been carried out by Christopher Catherwood, the Doctor's eldest grandchild and Editorial Director of Crossway Books in England. Elizabeth Catherwood, the Doctor's elder daughter, has gone through them carefully, to make sure that all the editing has been faithful to the Doctor himself. To her, as always, go the very warmest thanks for all the work that she has done. Full thanks are also due to Alison Walley, for preparing the transcript for publication, and not least because of her wonderful ability to read the handwriting of the Doctor's descendants, the editor's not being dissimilar in legibility to the Doctor's own . . .

Renewed thanks must go to the team at Crossway USA. Once again, prime thanks are due to Lane Dennis for his commitment to the Doctor's work. Some have spoken of a renaissance of interest in the books of Martyn Lloyd-Jones in recent years, and there is no doubt that the work of Crossway Books, under the leadership of Lane Dennis, has been a major factor in that growth. Warm thanks are also due to Fred Rudy, Len Goss, and Ted Griffin. Backroom editors like Ted do not always get the credit they deserve, and so it is a pleasure to give it here. Crossway USA shares the love for God's Word that the Doctor had, and it shows.

NOTE TO READERS

When we came to editing this volume, we discovered that one of the transcripts early on in the series on 1 John 4 was missing, and a search among the duplicate set in Scotland confirmed this. However, we decided that the Doctor's sermons on this chapter remain so powerful that we should go ahead and publish them anyway. Dr. Lloyd-Jones often recapitulated his previous sermon at the beginning of the next, and so the reader can in fact partly discover what he said in the missing sermon in this way.

As readers of volume 2 of Iain Murray's biography of Dr. Lloyd-Jones will remember, the Doctor had some major spiritual experiences during 1949. One can get a flavour of this by the sermons in this book, preached mainly just after the events which Iain Murray describes. It is easy to see why Jim Packer felt that the Doctor at this time was on a 'plateau of supreme excellence.' As all the sermons were faithfully transcribed at the time, we can enjoy them now, and can be as challenged and encouraged to hear of the love of God for His people as were those in the congregation of Westminster Chapel to whom they were preached.

1
Test the Spirits

Beloved, believe not every spirit, but try the spirits whether they are of God: because many false prophets are gone out into the world.

1 JOHN 4:1

As we begin our consideration of the fourth chapter of this first epistle of John, perhaps it would be helpful if I would remind you very briefly of our understanding in general of the teaching of this epistle. When we began to consider it,[1] I reminded you that many have analysed this epistle, and that it is almost impossible to find any two who agree in their analysis. So we decided that we had as good a right as anybody else to offer our own analysis of the epistle, and we have been looking at it in this way.

The great theme of the Apostle is the possibility of having joy in this world, a joy that comes from God, in spite of circumstances and conditions. John has made that perfectly plain, it seems to me, in the fourth verse of the first chapter: 'And these things write we unto you, that your joy may be full.' That is what he is concerned about, and that is the extraordinary thing which he unfolds to these people. They were Christians in a very difficult and gainsaying world, and yet John, now an old man, writes to them to say that although 'the whole world lieth in wickedness,' nevertheless it is possible for them to have a joy, a fullness of joy, in spite of it all.

And we have been suggesting that he says that there are two great and main things which as Christians we have to remember and hold on to, come what may. The first is that we have fellowship with God; that the main effect of the coming of the Lord Jesus Christ into this world, and of His work, is that we who believe on Him and belong to Him and are in Him have fellowship with God; we are walking with God. The second great thing is that we, as children of God, not only have fellowship with Him, but we are in that relationship which makes us children.

Now this question of fellowship is the one which is dealt with in chapters 1, 2 and 3 and until verse 6 of the fourth chapter. John has been dealing with the condition and position of being children—that we are sons of God. 'Those two things,' says John in effect, and he keeps on repeating it, 'you must never lose hold of: first, you are walking with God, and your fellowship is with the Father and with His Son Jesus Christ, and, second, you are the children of God.' But, you will remember that he, as a very practical and wise teacher, is not content merely to make general statements like that. He has his own experience, and he knows perfectly well from that, leave alone from his handling of other Christian people, that there are certain things in this life and world which always tend to militate against our enjoyment of this joy. There are things which would always try to break our fellowship with God, and there are things which will tend at any rate to make us less conscious of the fact that we are the children of God. So he has been dealing at length with these things.

Now it is interesting to observe that these things which militate against fellowship are exactly the same things which militate against sonship, and we have been dealing with them.[2] There are three main things which we have to watch. The first is that we must keep the commandments; if we want to enjoy fellowship with God we must obey Him, we must keep His commandments. You will find that John deals with that at the beginning of the second chapter. The second thing is that we must love one another; we must 'love the brethren.' And the third thing is that we must beware of false teaching. There are antichrists, there are enemies of the faith, and we must be absolutely clear and certain as to what we believe, and especially about our belief about the Lord Jesus Christ himself.

Then at the beginning of chapter 3, John comes to the second great point, that we are children of God. 'Behold, what manner of love the Father hath bestowed upon us, that we should be called the sons of God'; and he tells us about that. He then goes on to say in effect, 'If you want to live in full enjoyment of that sonship, there are certain things you must beware of. You must obey the law– "whosoever commiteth sin transgresseth also the law"'–and the first verses of chapter 3 emphasise the all-importance of obeying the commandments.

Having done that, he goes on to remind them of brotherly love: 'In this the children of God are manifest, and the children of the devil: whosoever doeth not righteousness is not of God, neither he that loveth not his brother. For this is the message that ye heard from the beginning, that we should love one another.'

Then here in the first verse of chapter 4, we come to a continuation of the theme on which John had started at the end of the previous chapter: 'Hereby we know that he abideth in us, by the Spirit which he hath given us.'[3] And we have seen that we are undoubtedly face to face with one of the most important matters in the whole realm of our Christian faith and profession. Not only that, we are also confronted by one of the most difficult subjects in connection with our Christian faith and one which has consequently led often to much discussion and dispute, not to say controversy and bitterness.

The way in which the Apostle deals with it seems to me to be thoroughly typical and characteristic of the Scripture. Indeed, I always feel that one of the most glorious things about Scripture is this extraordinary balance, and that is what always strikes one at once as one comes across a statement like this. 'Hereby we know that he abideth in us, by the Spirit which he hath given us. Beloved, believe not every spirit, but try the spirits whether they are of God.'

Now this is very characteristic of the scriptural method; indeed, had the Church, and had Christian people, always been careful to observe this perfection of balanced statements, then much of the controversy to which I have referred, and certainly much of the bitterness, would have been entirely avoided. But the trouble with us as the result of sin is that we always seem to delight in extremes, and we tend to go from one extreme to the other instead of maintaining the position of scriptural balance. That seems to be the tendency of mankind, and perhaps it has never manifested itself more, and more often, than concerning this very subject which faces us as we look at this verse. The subject is the whole problem of the place of the Holy Spirit in Christian experience. Or if you prefer, there is a more particular problem here, and that is the problem of the respective places of experience and doctrine in the Christian life: experience, doctrine, and the Holy Spirit.

Now the trouble has generally been due to the fact that people have emphasised either experience or doctrine at the expense of the other, and indeed they have often been guilty, and still are, of putting up as contrasts things which clearly are meant to be complementary. This is something which has been happening in the Church almost from the very beginning. There was a great deal of this in the early years of this present century. Many books were published then, nearly all of them dealing with this subject; one of the books was called *Religions of Theology and Religions of the Spirit*, and that was the vogue at the time, to compare these things which were put up as contrasts. It was said that your religion must either be a religion based upon some authoritative doctrinal, dogmatic teaching, or else it was one of those 'free religions of the Spirit,' and the one was generally put up against the other.

This is something which could be dealt with very easily from the historical standpoint, though we shall not do this at any length.

But the whole difficulty is this tendency to oscillate between two extreme positions instead of combining the two. These are those who tend to emphasise the work and influence of the Spirit. They emphasise experience at the expense of doctrine and of truth. They say, 'But doesn't the Scripture say, "We know he abideth in us, by the Spirit which he hath given us"? It is not your authorities, not your creeds and definitions, but something alive and living–the religion of the Spirit!' But then you have people on the other side who have said, 'Yes, that is all right, but what the Scripture really says is this: "Believe not every spirit, but try the spirits whether they be of God."'

And thus when the whole emphasis is placed upon one or the other, you have either a tendency to fanaticism and excesses or a tendency toward a barren intellectualism and a mechanical and a dead kind of orthodoxy. That is the position put more or less in general. It is all the result of putting the whole emphasis on one or the other instead of seeing that the two are essential. It is the thing about which the Apostle Paul was contending with the church at Corinth, the whole idea of identifying the complete body; they were tending to think of the separate parts instead of realising this balance which is always a great characteristic of life.

This is a problem which can be illustrated perfectly at particular points of history. It was in a sense the problem with which the early church herself had to contend. There was a grave danger that the whole of the Christian faith, the balance of the truth and of the gospel and of the faith, might have been entirely upset as the result of the activity of certain people. It was exactly what John was writing about in this epistle. There were certain people who claimed unusual authority from God, who claimed to have the Spirit in an unusual and marked manner and were impatient of teaching and definition and doctrine. And the great fight for the faith which was fought in this early century was against this tendency, *for* the apostolic teaching and authority and *against* those who talked more in terms of the special authority which they had received and of the Spirit's guidance of which they said they were the recipients.

We see, of course, exactly the same thing at the time of the Reformation. Luther and Calvin and others as the result of their wonderful experience, as the result of what the Spirit of God had done to them, renounced the teaching of the medieval Church. They began to preach a living gospel and faith, but almost immediately after they had started doing so they were confronted by a new and fresh problem. The Reformation immediately led to a whole host of new sects, led by people who were claiming some immediate revelation, those who spoke, as they claimed, by the inspiration of the Spirit and were guilty of all kinds of excesses. As you read the stories of Luther and Calvin and other Reformation Fathers, you will find that they began to fight this war on two fronts. They were fighting a dead, mechanical intellectualism on one hand, and they had to fight these other people who were running to excess and riot on the other.

Then in the seventeenth century you find the same kind of thing in connection with the Puritan movement. It is one of the most fascinating bits of history to read the story of the fight that went on within the ranks of Puritanism itself. There were three main sections. There were those who eventually became the Quakers, who exhorted the doctrine of the 'Inner Light' and immediate experience, and who were rather negligent of the Word itself and all examining and testing. That was one extreme. Then on the other hand you had those who became guilty of a kind of intellectualism, who discounted the Spirit altogether, who were concerned about the more or less legalistic statements of the truth. Then in the middle you had people like the great Dr. John Owen, and Thomas Goodwin in London, who constantly emphasised what they regarded as the only true scriptural position—namely, the one we have here, the position which emphasises Spirit and doctrine, experience and definition. You must not say it is either/or; it is both. These, too, had to wage a warfare constantly on the two fronts;

they had to fight the dead, barren intellectualism of many in Anglicanism and in the ranks of Puritanism, and the wild excesses of the early Quakers and various others who troubled them not a little.

That is a brief history survey. 'But,' someone may say, 'that is all right, and no doubt if we were living in the sixteenth or seventeenth centuries, or in the early centuries, this may have been very important for us. But surely by now this has become quite remote. It is just academic. No doubt some of you rejoice in reading about things like that, it is your particular hobby, but what has it to do with us?'

I suggest that in many ways it is one of the most acute problems confronting the Church at the present time. So let us look at it like this: I maintain that in those who take their Christian faith and religion at all seriously, there are still these two tendencies manifested at the present time. Alas, I am sure it is true to say of the vast majority that they are utterly indifferent to true doctrine—they are concerned only about supporting the mechanism of the Church. They seem to be quite unconcerned about these things, and because of their lack of interest in doctrine, their one idea is to establish a great world Church without any doctrine whatsoever. But amongst those who really are alive and alert, these two ancient tendencies are still manifesting themselves.

There is what I would call a movement to a kind of new orthodoxy; I am anxious to avoid mentioning names, and yet it is more or less essential that I should do so. There is that movement which is known as Barthianism, which is merely concerned about doctrine and spends most of its time in teaching doctrine. There we see the tendency to pure intellectualism, a concern about truth in the abstract, about definitions and ideas, and to stop at that. But then there is another movement, and there is always this opposite movement. There is a great tendency on the part of many to stress only the experimental side—the experiencing side, and to talk only about the gifts of the Spirit and the various manifestations of life and religion, as they call it.

My point is that those who really are concerned about these matters are still tending to take up one or the other of these positions. As I understand it, the position of those of us who claim to be Evangelical is nothing but a repetition of that of the Protestant Fathers and that of certain of the leaders of the Puritan Movement in the seventeenth century. As Evangelicals we find ourselves fighting on two fronts. We are obviously critical of a pure intellectualism and of a dead mechanical Church which lacks any life. We are here to say that 'Hereby we know that he abideth in us, by the Spirit which he hath given us.' We say, 'It is not enough for people to be church members.' We ask, 'Are they born again? Have they evidence within them of the life of God in their soul?' We say we are not concerned about a mere theoretical belief; the gospel of Jesus Christ is a life-giving gospel. That is one side; but on the other side we see certain tendencies and we see certain excesses and we say, 'Believe not every spirit, but try the spirits whether they are of God.' And thus we seem to be opposing everything, and so we receive criticisms from all sides.

Now we are not concerned merely about our own position; we are concerned primarily about the truth. But let me say this. It seems to me that we have a right to be fairly happy about ourselves as long as we have criticism from both sides; but if the criticism should ever stop on one side, then is the time to be careful. For myself, as long as I am charged by certain people with being nothing but a Pentecostalist and on the other hand charged by others with being an intellectual, a man who is always preaching doctrine, as long as the two criticisms come, I am very happy. But if one or the other of the two criticisms should ever cease, then, I say, is the time to be careful and to begin to examine the very foundations.

The position of the Scripture, as I am trying to show you, is one which is facing two extremes; the Spirit is essential, and experience is vital; however, truth and definition and doctrine and dogma are equally vital and essential. And our whole position is one which proclaims that experience which is not based solidly upon truth and doctrine is dangerous. That, then, is a comprehensive general statement, but now let us look at it in detail as it is presented to us here by the Apostle. Let me divide it up in this way:

First of all, there is the necessity for testing and trying the spirits. 'Beloved, believe not every spirit, but try the spirits whether they are of God.' Now there are some people who object root and branch to this process of testing. There are many reasons for that, of course. In the case of some people it is nothing but slackness, indolence, and laziness—a desire for ease. Religion? 'Ah,' they say, 'you must not always be arriving at your definitions and examining and testing.' They dislike the whole thing; they just want to go on as they have always done. I do not think we need to discuss them further—there is no excuse for such an attitude.

Then there are others who seem to object to this process of testing because they are what we may call 'anti-theological.' It is amazing how many people who claim the name *Christian* are actively opposed to theology; they dislike it and say, 'I am not interested in theology. All I believe is that a man should do this, that, and the other'; they look askance upon definition and dogmas. Well, all I can say to such people is that their first duty is to read the history of the Christian Church and the lives of the saints. Indeed, they can start by reading the New Testament itself, and they will find that it is essentially theological; it is our duty to understand the truth we claim to believe, in order that we may state and express it in such a manner that God can use it for the salvation of others.

But there are those who feel that this whole process of testing and trying the spirits is something unscriptural. I am not anxious to caricature such people, but they do take up that position. The scriptural person, according to their idea, is one who, as it were, lives with his head in the clouds and must never come down to earth on matters of definition; and the moment you begin to discuss and consider and debate and define, you cease to be a purely spiritual person. A spiritual person, according to such ideas, is some ethereal being who really must not be bothering with these mechanical and mundane matters of definition.

And then there are those who object to such testing because they say that surely the only thing that matters is that people should be honest and sincere; and if people are absolutely sincere about these things, then their doctrine will look after itself.

Now there is a great deal of this spirit abroad—an objection to testing and trying the spirits. I remember a man saying to me on one occasion, after I had made a brief reference to this matter, 'I am not interested in what you are saying. The great question is, are you being used?' In other words, it does not matter what I say in terms of truth so long as I feel something and experience something—that is the attitude. But my reply to this is that we must test and try the spirits because Scripture commands and exhorts us to do so, and for me that is enough. 'Beloved, believe not every spirit, but try the spirits.' This is a commandment, and I have no right to put it aside.

Not only that, but Scripture tells us why we ought to do so— 'because many false prophets are gone out into the world.' The Scripture tells us that 'We wrestle not against flesh and blood, but against principalities, against powers, against the rulers of the darkness of this world, against spiritual wickedness in high places' (Eph 6:12). Alas, there are false prophets; there are evil spirits; there is a devil who is so clever and subtle that he can transform himself into an angel of light. If we were confronted with the Holy Spirit only, there would be no need to test the spirits, but the very name '*Holy* Spirit' suggests other spirits, devilish spirits—and there are such powers.

The third reason for testing and trying is the evidence provided by the long history of the church of the havoc that has often been wrought in the Church because people would not try and test the spirits—because they said, 'I have received such a wonderful experience, and therefore I must be right.' But for the reasons I have given for definition and dogma and examination, the whole history of the church presses us and urges us to test and to try and to follow the scriptural injunction. In other words, what we are concerned about is not a matter only of sincerity and honesty—we are concerned about truth and error, and truth and error is something which has to be defined.

But let me ask a second question: Is this something only for theologians and professors of theology or perhaps for ministers and leaders? Is it only for certain people? And the answer is that it is for *all*. 'Beloved'—he is writing to the average church member—'believe not every spirit, but try the spirits.' Later on he says, 'Ye are of God, little children' (v 4), and I think he used the expression 'little children' deliberately— 'you, the ordinary church members, little children—you hear us because you are of the truth.'

It is the duty and the business of everyone claiming the name *Christian* to be in a position to try and examine and test the spirits. Indeed, we are given the power to do so—'greater is he that is in you, than he that is in the world' (v 4). We have been given this capacity by God, through the Holy Spirit; the Spirit dwells in us, and therefore we have this power of discrimination and understanding. The Apostle Paul tells us that at great length in 1 Corinthians. For example, 'We have received, not the spirit of the world, but the Spirit which is of God; that we might know the things that are freely given to us of God' (2:12). That is it!

Then I come to the last and vital question: How is this testing to be done? How are we to know whether certain spirits are true or false? Let me mention, first of all, tests which are dangerous if we rely upon them only, and let me first put it in general.

There are those who claim that the gifts of the Spirit are absolutely essential, and that unless men and women are able to manifest certain gifts of the Spirit, they have not received the Spirit. They say, for example, 'You have not received the Holy Spirit unless you are able to speak in tongues, or have done this or that.' They refer to a particular gift, and they say that if you have not experienced that, you have not received the Spirit, in spite of the fact that the Apostle Paul asks the question, 'Do all speak with tongues?' (1 Cor 12:30). The whole of that chapter is designed to show that the gifts are distributed by the Lord Himself. He may or may not give these gifts, and the manifestation of gifts is not an essential proof of the possession of the Spirit.[4]

But let me go on to particular matters. A very dangerous way of testing or examining the claim to having the Spirit is to judge in terms of phenomena, as in the gift of healing, or the particular result of a ministry. These are the tests that are put up. People say, 'Surely this man must be right. Haven't you heard what he has been doing? Haven't you heard of the cures he is able to bring about. Look at the results he has had.' The test of phenomena, taken alone, is an extremely dangerous one because evil spirits can work miracles; our Lord warned His followers that these spirits would be able to do such marvelous works.

Let me give you a piece of historical evidence. A man by the name of John Brown, who was a surgeon to King Charles II, published a book in 1684 bearing the title *Scrofula treated by the touch of Kings*, and these extraordinary facts are therein revealed: From 1660-1662 Charles II laid his hands upon 90,000 people suffering from scrofula—a tubercular disease of the glands of the neck. The man who writes the book was a surgeon, and he says he has evidence to prove that in at least fifty of the cases the cures were miraculous. Charles II had the gift of healing! I pass that on as a piece of evidence which is well worth our consideration.

The same applies to fervour; the fact that people are full of fervour does not imply that they have the Holy Spirit. Evil spirits are often very fervent. Great excitement is not a proof of the Spirit; great energy is not a proof of the Spirit; much assurance or confidence is not a proof of the Spirit. How often the only tests and the true tests taken are that a man speaks with confidence and assurance and that he is energetic. I would to God that energy in a man's preaching was proof of the power of the Spirit, but, alas, I know it is not; the flesh can evidence false feelings, and to put that up as a test is dangerous.

It is likewise with the test of experience. People may come and say they have had visions; they have had most extraordinary dreams. They say that strange things have happened to them; they have had unusual guidance, astonishing answers to prayer. 'I prayed,' says a man, 'and this happened,' and we tend to say this man must be full of the Spirit. Experience! But believe me, such experiences can be counterfeited by the enemy and often have been; experiences have come and do come to us, but let us not rest on them, and let us not put up the test of experience as the sole test.

So, if we reject those tests, then what are the true tests? Let me first just note them.

The first and the most important test is conformity to scriptural teaching. Try the spirits; test the spirits. 'Hereby know ye the Spirit of God: Every spirit that confesseth that Jesus Christ is come in the flesh is of God' (v 2). How do I know that this is a spiritual test? All I know about Him I put up to the test of Scripture. Indeed, you get exactly the same thing in the sixth verse where John says, speaking of himself and the other Apostles, 'We are of God: he that knoweth God heareth us; he that is not of God heareth not us. Hereby know we the spirit of truth, and the spirit of error.' The first thing to ask about a man who claims to be filled with the Spirit and to be an unusual teacher is, does his teaching conform to Scripture? Is it in conformity with the apostolic message? Does he base it all upon this Word? Is he willing to submit to it? That is the great test.

But I want to emphasise this next one: A readiness to listen to scriptural teaching and to abide by it is always a characteristic of the true prophet. You will find that the other man rather tends to dismiss it. 'Ah yes,' he says, 'but you are legalistic, you are just a theologian; I have experienced, I have felt, and I have produced this and that.' The tendency is not to abide by the teaching of Scripture but to be almost contemptuous of it; that has always been the characteristic of those who have tended to go astray. Read the history of the Quakers, and you find that such an attitude became a prominent feature—the inner light rather than the objective teaching of Scripture itself.

But, of course, and this is the greatest test, the true Spirit always glorifies Christ; He is always in the centre; He is always given the pre-eminence. And the true prophet is not the man who talks about experiences and visions and what he has done and seen, but about Christ. And when you have heard him you do not say, 'What a wonderful man'; you say, 'What a wonderful Saviour!' You do not say, 'What a wonderful experience this man has had'; you say, 'Who is the Man of whom he is speaking?' The attraction is to Christ; he glorifies Christ.

The last thing I would mention is that with which I started—the perfect balance. 'God,' said Paul to Timothy 'hath not given us the spirit of fear; but of power, and of love, and of a sound mind' (2 Tim 1:7). This is discipline, balance. The man who has the Holy Spirit is the man who always manifests balance and proportion. 'Be not drunk with wine, wherein is excess; but be filled with the Spirit' (Eph 5:18); there is power and balance, but no excess. Speak one at a time, says Paul to the people of Corinth. 'But,' they say, 'we cannot. Isn't that quenching the Spirit?' 'No,' says Paul, 'let all things be done . . . in order' (see 1 Cor 14:33, 40). The Holy Spirit is the Spirit of order, not of disorder. Doctrine and love are required; experience and power, intellect and mind—the whole person is involved and functions as this perfectly balanced body with no schism, with no rivalry and competition, but with the whole manifesting and ministering unto the glory of the Lord and Saviour, Jesus Christ.

We have only been able to deal briefly with this subject which, as I have said, is a great one. 'Beloved, believe not every spirit, but try the spirits.' I say, make sure you have the Spirit. It is 'hereby we know that he abideth in us, by the Spirit which he hath given us.' Make sure the Spirit of God is in you, and then make sure that it is the Spirit of God and not some false, evil spirit to whom you are listening.

2
The All-sufficiency of Christ

> Hereby know ye the Spirit of God: Every spirit that confesseth that Jesus Christ is come in the flesh is of God: and every spirit that confesseth not that Jesus Christ is come in the flesh is not of God: and this is that spirit of antichrist, whereof ye have heard that it should come; and even now already is it in the world.
>
> 1 JOHN 4:2-3

Here in these two verses John emphasises what is, after all, the ultimate test in this matter of trying and testing the spirits. We have considered a number of general tests, and, in an attempt to give a fairly comprehensive list, I mentioned in passing that one of the most valuable and thorough tests always is whether such a teaching or such a person glorifies the Lord Jesus Christ.

Now in these two verses we have to return to that, and John appeals to us to do so. It is not enough just to say in general that a teaching should glorify the Lord Jesus Christ; we must know what we mean by that. And, indeed, the whole epistle, in a sense, is nothing but one great repetition of the Apostle concerning this central and vital matter.

So let me try to summarise this by putting it in the form of a number of principles, and let me say in passing that this is the note on which Christian preaching should always begin and should always end. Let us look at it like this: The ultimate test of all who profess or teach Christianity is their attitude towards the Lord Jesus Christ. 'Hereby know ye the Spirit of God: Every spirit that confesseth that Jesus Christ is come in the flesh is of God: and every spirit that confesseth not that Jesus Christ is come in the flesh is not of God'; whatever their gifts may be and however wonderful they may be, they are not of God; 'and this is that spirit of antichrist, whereof ye have heard that it should come; and even now already is it in the world.'

So this is the infallible test. John goes on repeating it, and we must continue to do so. The Lord Jesus Christ is absolutely vital, central, and essential to the Christian position, and I do not hesitate, therefore, to aver that any teaching in which the Lord Jesus Christ is not in that position is not true Christian teaching, whatever else it may be. Now let me try to enforce that by putting it in terms of a number of negative statements.

Christianity is not a mystical feeling or experience only. I put it like that because there is a good deal of interest in that kind of experience at the present time. I think you always tend to get a return to mysticism at a time of crisis or of difficulty in the history of the world. When men and women see all other powers fail on all hands, when they see that all the optimistic prophets and teachers and politicians and poets have been entirely wrong, when they are troubled and bewildered and perplexed, there is always some kind of innate tendency in men and women to turn to mysticism. People nowadays talk about 'getting in tune with the heart of the universe'; they talk about 'getting in touch with the Unseen.' There is also a considerable revival of Buddhism at the present time. Certain popular well-known novelists, people like Mr. Aldous

Huxley[1] and others, who once claimed to be pure intellectuals, are now saying, one after another, that the only hope for this world is mysticism, and the mysticism that they are interested in is Buddhism.

There is, indeed, a revival of interest in these so-called 'Eastern religions.' People, in a kind of desperation, are anxious to get back into something that is eternal and unseen, and there are many people who think that anybody who is at all interested in these things is automatically a Christian. 'Ah,' they say, 'I used to be quite materialistic, and I was only interested in the things I could see, but I have developed a great interest in the unseen and in the spiritual'; and so they have become interested in experiences and feelings along the mystical line.

Now there *is* a mystical element in the gospel of Jesus Christ, and it is very practical and experimental. But here I would emphasise that a mere vague, general interest in the unseen and the spiritual does not make one a Christian. Spiritism can do that, and so can Buddhism and most of the other religions. But that is not the Christian position.

Or let me put it to you like this: Merely to claim that one has a new sense of power in one's life does not prove that one is a Christian. There is also a great deal of interest in these days in this sense of power. People say, 'My life had gone to pieces. I became conscious that I lacked power. But now I believe that there is a new power in my life; I am able to do what I could not do before.' And many people believe that to say such a thing is proof positive that one has become a Christian. But the simple answer is that there are many agencies that can do that; Christian Science does it, psychology does it—it is a part of such religion.

I once read a book by a man in which he stated this whole position. He was an author, a playwright, and he pointed out that the big mistake he had been making in his professional life was that he has used the higher part of his brain too much. There he was with his mind as it were sweating and straining, and then he said, 'I made this marvelous discovery,' and it happened to him as the result of some experience that he had. 'I found,' he said, 'that the great thing to do was not to use the active part of my brain, but to use the lower part of my brain.' He went on to describe the ease with which he now wrote. He allowed the lower part of the brain to rule his life for him, and he was conscious of some strange, extraordinary power. There are many who are interested in power in life. There *is* a great and glorious power in the Christian faith, but merely to be able to claim we have a new power in our life does not prove we are Christians.

Let me even say that the Christian position is not just one in which we subscribe to a number of exalted teachings and ideas. Here again you will find that this idea is very frequent. People say, 'I have gone on for years, and I have never been interested in these elevated thoughts and ideas of life, but now I *am* interested in them'; and having subscribed to this elevated conception of life, they think they have become Christians. But there are many elevated teachings. You can find them in Greek pagan philosophy or in many modern philosophies; but these thoughts and ideas alone are not Christianity.

Indeed, I do not hesitate to go as far as this: Even to accept the teaching of the Lord Jesus Christ, just as teaching, does not make one a Christian. The whole emphasis of this epistle, as of the whole of the New Testament, is on the person Himself. It is possible for people to take up certain parts of the teaching of Christ and to praise it. A man like Mahatma Gandhi did that. He was not a Christian, but he praised the teaching of Christ and told people they ought to try to practise it. Merely to praise the teaching of Christ does not make one a Christian. No; the emphasis is upon the person Himself, and upon our relationship to Him. 'Hereby know ye the Spirit of God: Every spirit that confesseth that Jesus Christ is come in the flesh is of God.'

But now this leads to a further careful definition, and that, of course, is because of these antichrists about whom John is speaking. It is not enough even for people to say they believe on the Lord Jesus Christ; we must know something of what they mean by that. After all, John is here reminding these people that there were those in the early church who said that they believed in the Lord Jesus Christ and yet were false prophets, antichrists, false teachers.

Definition is absolutely essential. That is why any people who say that they are not interested in theology and doctrine are not only unscriptural, they are ignorant; they are denying the Scriptures. So it is very important that we should be clear about these things, because of the teaching of antichrists. Perhaps the best way to put that clearly is to remind ourselves of what we saw when we considered this question of the antichrists in the second chapter.[2] The antichrists did not completely deny the Lord Jesus Christ. That was not the trouble with them. A teaching which denies the whole of the teaching of the Lord Jesus Christ is self-evident and is to that extent not a danger. That is why I never agree with people that the main danger confronting the church is something like communism. No, the greatest danger is always something within, and these antichrists were within the church.

What is the teaching of the antichrist? It is not a denial of Christ; it is a misrepresentation of Christ; it is a teaching that either does something to Him or detracts something from Him. You remember how John put it; he said these people 'went out from us, but they were not of us: for if they had been of us, they would no doubt have continued with us; but they went out, that they might be manifest that they were not all of us' (2:19). They were in the church. The antichrists had arisen *within* the Christian church; they said they believed in Christ, and yet, says John, their teaching is such that we can prove that they do not truly believe in Him.

Now this is a very important principle to grasp. Merely for people to say, 'Yes, I believe in the Lord Jesus Christ; I always have believed in Him,' is not enough, until we have tested them further. The Apostle Paul says that these people preach 'another Jesus.' Ah, yes, they were preaching Jesus, but it was *another* Jesus; it was not the Jesus that Paul preached (2 Cor 11:4). They preached Christ, yes, but what sort of a Christ, what kind of a Jesus? That is the question.

Therefore we ask this question: How can we decide whether the teaching concerning Jesus Christ is true or false? And here the one answer is given perfectly clearly. Our ultimate authority, our only authority, is the apostolic teaching. Now that is the whole point of this first epistle of John. In a sense this is what he is saying from beginning to end. 'Go on believing,' says John, 'what I and my fellow Apostles have taught you and have told you.' There were these other people who claimed wonderful gifts, they seemed to be doing extraordinary things, they had some sort of spirit in them, and they were claiming authoritative teaching. But John's whole purpose in writing was to say to these early Christians, 'Hold on to what I and the other Apostles have told you.'

You remember how he began? 'That which was from the beginning, which we have heard, which we have seen with our eyes, which we have looked upon, and our hands have handled, of the Word of life.' He is referring to the Apostles, and he says that he writes these things that these Christians 'may have fellowship with *us*.' Who are they? They are still the Apostles.

Now this is something which is absolutely primary and fundamental. The claim of the New Testament is that it alone is authoritative in these matters. It teaches us that the Apostles and Prophets were the people to whom God, through the Holy Spirit, had revealed spiritual truth, and He meant them to teach it in word and to write it. The Apostle Paul tells us in Ephesians 2:20 that the Christian Church is 'built upon the foundation of the apostles and prophets.' All teaching must derive from them, and so you have this extraordinary claim in the New Testament. These men claimed a unique authority.

Listen to the Apostle Paul putting it again in writing to the Galatians; he uses strong language like this: 'But though we, or an angel from heaven, preach any other gospel unto you than that which we have preached unto you, let him be accursed' (Gal 1:8). 'What egotism!' says someone. No, it is not egotism; it is the claim of a man who has been commissioned by God. God has set him apart; God has given him the revelation. And he goes on to argue in so many of his letters that what he preached was also the message that was preached by the other Apostles. This Apostle and all the other Apostles do not hesitate to say that they exhorted these people to test every teaching by their teaching. In other words, you and I are still committed to the same position. We are to judge teaching not by the experience it gives, not by anything flashy or spectacular that may characterize it. It is not enough, John says, to name Christ. The question is, does the teaching conform to the teaching of the New Testament concerning the person of our Lord and Saviour Jesus Christ or does it not? That is the test.

That leads to the next question. What is this apostolic teaching concerning Him? Now in a phrase in our text John gives us the perfect answer. John does not use words like this haphazardly. Listen to the way in which he puts it: 'Hereby know ye the Spirit of God: Every spirit that confesseth that Jesus Christ is come in the flesh is of God: and every spirit that confesseth not that Jesus Christ is come in the flesh is not of God.' Now here is the statement: *'Jesus Christ is come in the flesh'*; Jesus Christ arrived in the world 'in the flesh.' What does this mean? Let me try to show you how John in putting it like that was countering and answering some of those grievous heresies that had already arisen even in his day in the church, before the end of the first century.

Take the expression 'Jesus Christ.' Why does John say *'Jesus Christ* is come in the flesh'? Why did he not say that Jesus or that Christ has come in the flesh? Ah, that is most important; that is his way of emphasising the unity of the blessed person. The Lord Jesus Christ is one person, but He has two natures—the divine and the human; and yet there is only one person. Now as we have seen in the earlier chapters of 1 John,[3] there were false prophets, the antichrists in the early church, and some of them said something like this: Jesus of Nazareth was just a man like every other man, but when He was baptised by John in the Jordan, the eternal Christ came upon Him and began to use Him; and the eternal Christ continued with the man Jesus until He came to the cross. But on the cross the eternal Christ went away, back to heaven, and it was only the man Jesus who died. There were two persons—the man Jesus and the eternal Christ. No! says John; '*Jesus Christ*,' one person but two natures—the two natures in one person.

The history of the church shows very clearly the vital importance of emphasising this. All the subsequent heresies with regard to the person of our Lord arose in the first few centuries. Someone put this very well when they said, 'The canon of infidelity was closed about exactly the same time as the canon of Scripture was closed.' That is a very interesting statement. There is no modern heresy. All the clever people who propound their apparently new ideas about Christ are simply repeating what has already been said; there have literally been no new heresies since the first centuries. But, you see, men have constantly fallen into that error; some have seen God only, and others have seen man only, and others have tried to see the two. That is why we must never say Jesus is God, Jesus is man; no, Jesus Christ is the God-man. In the Incarnation, the eternal Son of God took our nature unto Himself deliberately; He is the God-man, Jesus Christ.

Let me hold another phrase before you: 'Jesus Christ *is come*.' What a significant statement! Do you see what it implies? It suggests that He was before; He has come from somewhere. It could be said of no one else that he has come into this world and into this life. You and I are born, but He *came*. John, as I have already reminded you, has already said at the commencement of the epistle, 'That which was from the beginning'; that is it! This eternal life has been manifested. He is still talking about the eternal Son of God who has come into this world; he is describing the whole miracle and marvel and wonder of the Incarnation. That is the theme; He is come.

You get this in so many places in Scripture: 'This is the condemnation, that the light *is come* into the world' (John 3:19); 'Unto you that fear my name shall the Sun of righteousness arise with healing in his wings' (Mal 4:2). All these phrases are pointing in the same direction, so that as we look at the person of the Lord Jesus Christ we must be absolutely confident and sure that we do verily believe that that person, that babe in the manger, is the one who has come from the realms of glory—no one else, none other. 'Jesus Christ is come'; He has entered into the world. He is a visitor from another realm; He has erupted into history. That is the idea. So you see John was not using a casual phrase when he said, 'Jesus Christ is come.' There were people already denying His Godhead, His unique Deity, His eternal Sonship, and here John is emphasising it.

Even further, he says, 'Jesus Christ is come *in the flesh*.' In other words, the eternal Son did not have a mere phantom body. People had taught that. Some of those antichrists, those first heretics, said, 'Yes, the person described as Jesus is the eternal Christ, the eternal Son of God, but you must not talk about the Incarnation. You must not say, "the Word was made flesh," you must not say He has come in the flesh. What happened,' they said, 'was that He took upon Himself a kind of phantom, ethereal body. What happened was something similar to those theophanies when the Angel of the Covenant suddenly appeared to Abraham or somebody else, a temporary appearance of the eternal Son, not a real incarnation.'

'Avoid that heresy,' says John, 'as you value your souls and as you value the faith. Jesus Christ is come *in the flesh*.' 'The Word was made flesh, and dwelt among us' (John 1:14). He was born as a baby in Bethlehem. He grew 'in wisdom and stature, and in favor with God and man' (Luke 2:52). His humanity is absolutely real; may we never lose hold of that. 'Jesus Christ is come in the flesh'— this is the actuality of the Incarnation.

Why is John so concerned about all this? Why is he so careful to define what he believes about the Lord Jesus Christ in such detail and in such minute accuracy? It was all because of the false teachings that were then current and have been current ever since. What was the matter with them? All these false teachings were somehow or other detracting from Christ. Some were detracting from the glory of His person. Some said He was only a man, a wonderful man, the greatest religious genius of all time, one who was given the Holy Spirit in an exceptional degree and was therefore able to teach. Indeed as one has put it, 'Jesus achieved divinity.' Man only, but so wonderful that He, as it were, reached up and therefore will encourage us to follow His effort. Some therefore detract from Him by regarding Him as man only. Others detract from Him equally by regarding Him as God only. They would have us believe He is nothing but God appearing in a kind of cloak of flesh. Now each of these teachings detracts from Him because, let me emphasise again, He is not only man and not only God, but the astounding thing that has happened is that He is the God-man; He has taken humanity unto Himself.

But these false teachings detract also from the wonders of His works. And that is why John was so careful to emphasise that He is God 'in the flesh.' You see what it involves? If the Incarnation is not an actual fact, if He really has not been made flesh and dwelt among us, then there was no real humiliation involved in His coming into this world. He really did not limit Himself, as it were, to the position of a man dependent upon God; there is no real meaning in the laying aside of the insignia of the eternal glory; there is no true humiliation.

Furthermore, if He has not actually come in the flesh, there was no real suffering. If the eternal Christ left Him on the cross, the eternal Son of God did not suffer for the sins of mankind. There was no suffering at all in a sense; it was all appearance, it was all play-acting as it were. But I must go further. If it is not true to say that the eternal Son of God, having taken human nature unto Himself, has become the Lord Jesus Christ, if that glorious person in the unity of His person did not die upon that cross, then there is no atonement for sin, there is no expiation, and it is not true to say that He has tasted death for every man.

Yet that is what the New Testament claims for Him. It tells us that He was made for us 'a little lower than the angels . . . that he . . . should taste death for every man' (Heb 2:9). I say that if you are not clear about the Incarnation, you cannot believe that He has tasted death for you. How vital is this doctrine of the person of Jesus Christ! No man could die for my sins, and I say, with reverence, weighing my words, that God alone could not die for my sins. The Incarnation was essential, because we who need redemption are of the seed of Abraham. He has taken upon Himself this same nature, that as man He might die for our sins; and because He is the God-man, His dying is of eternal worth; thereby I am redeemed.

Do you see how important it is to contest and fight for these things? You cannot be a true Christian if you are unconcerned about the person of Jesus Christ and say, 'I do not understand these two natures in one person; I am not interested; I am not a theologian.' If you are not clear about this, you cannot be clear about your salvation. The Incarnation was essential because His death was essential. He came to die, and 'He died that we might be forgiven, he died to make us good'; He died to reconcile us to God.

In other words, the last point I am emphasising is that this false teaching detracts from the self-sufficiency of His work. You will find that so many of these false teachings talk about receiving power without mentioning Him at all. They claim wonderful power as the result of an experience, but they are detracting from the sufficiency of His work. They say, 'You must have an extra-special experience.' No, the teaching of the Scripture is that He alone is enough.

This teaching is as essential today as it was in the first century. Look, for example, at the place that some give to the Virgin Mary. I object to such teaching because it detracts from the all-sufficiency of my Lord. I do not need the assistance of the Virgin Mary. I speak with reverence: He and He alone is enough. I do not need to pray to the saints, because I have 'one mediator between God and men, the man Christ Jesus' (1 Tim 2:5). He needs no assistance. I am not dependent upon the sacraments for my salvation. I object to such teachings, for they detract from His unique and absolute all-sufficiency and comprehensiveness. The sacraments are of value, but they are not essential.

Let no one misunderstand me at this point. I am afraid I even object to teaching which emphasises the Holy Spirit at the expense of the person of the Son. The Holy Spirit was given in order that He might reveal the Son to me; the function of the Holy Spirit is not to call attention to Himself, but to direct attention to Christ, to present Him, to cause Him to dwell within us. Let us be careful that we do not emphasise even the Holy Spirit at the expense of the Son. The Son is alone, and He alone is enough.

What you and I are called upon to do as Christians I can put like this: We are to be ready to confess Him, and we are to do so gladly. Our confession is that He came into this world in order to save, that He alone can save me, and that He has done everything that is essential to my salvation. I need no other, and I will tolerate no other. He is central, He is enough, He is all and in all. 'Of him are ye in Christ Jesus, who of God is made unto us wisdom, and righteousness, and sanctification, and redemption' (1 Cor 1:30). Is there anything else you need? It is all in Him. In Him we are complete. Let us therefore give Him all the glory. 'Jesus Christ is come in the flesh'; He is enough. Let us therefore declare His death and His all-sufficiency until He comes again.

3
Born of God

> Beloved, let us love one another: for love is of God; and every one that loveth is born of God, and knoweth God. He that loveth not, knoweth not God; for God is love.
>
> 1 JOHN 4:7-8

Before we start on our consideration of these verses, I suggest to you that in my opinion John has really finished his active teaching at the end of verse 6 in this chapter, and that what we find after that is but a kind of reemphasis of what he has already been saying. There is no fresh doctrine from here on; he has laid down the two vital things—*fellowship* and *sonship*, and if we have these nothing can harm us.

But the man was such a wise teacher that, having said all that, he now ends with a *practical exhortation*; and the passage from the seventh verse in the fourth chapter to the end of verse 12 in the fifth chapter is just a repetition of these three things. And he starts with this particular matter of loving one another. He says, 'Beloved, let us love one another,' and he goes on with that theme until the first verse of the fifth chapter. Then from the second verse he goes back again to the all-importance of keeping the commandments; and from verse 5 to the end of verse 12 in the fifth chapter he returns to the correctness of belief, and especially to a correct belief concerning the person and work of the Lord Jesus Christ. Then from verse 13 to the end you have a kind of summary of the whole teaching.

Now I remind you of the scheme because it does help us to understand exactly what the Apostle has to say. So then, having done that, let us go back to this particular section, which begins with verse 7 in chapter 4 and goes to the end of verse 1 in chapter 5. John comes back once more to insist upon the vital importance of this demonstration of brotherly love. He has done it twice over, and he has been careful to go into details in his exposition of it, but still he comes back to it, and therefore I deduce that as the Apostle thus focuses upon this subject and dwells upon it and repeats it, it must be something which is of vital and paramount importance to him. It is interesting to observe that when he has finished his doctrine and direct exhortation, he puts this question of loving one another first.

This is characteristic of John. John is sometimes described as the Apostle of love. People say that Paul is the Apostle of faith, John the Apostle of love, and Peter the Apostle of hope; but I dislike these comparisons, because nothing on the subject of love has ever been written to compare with Paul's 1 Corinthians 13. Yet I suppose there is a sense in which there is something in such a distinction. However, it is very clear that this question of love is of vital importance, and John constantly emphasises it; and it is in connection with this that he says some of the most glorious and elevating things that can be found in the whole of Scripture. We have, for example, the great statement, 'God is love'; but it is the whole question of brotherly love that led him to say it. It was as he thought about this that he arrived at that great statement.

This, then, I would suggest, is indeed one of the things that is emphasised more than anything else in the whole of the New Testament. Our blessed Lord Himself at the very end of His ministry kept on repeating this same thing–'love one another.' He constantly told them that the world would be against them and that they would have tribulation. 'But,' he kept on saying, 'you love one another, and that is how the world will know that you are my disciples; this is the way in which you can demonstrate more clearly than anything else that you are my true followers and that you are children of God.' You will find this standing out in a most exceptional way if you read John 13–17.[1] But it is indeed a great theme running right through the entire New Testament—the Gospels and the Epistles.

I do not hesitate, therefore, to say that the ultimate test of our profession of the Christian faith is, I believe, this whole question of our loving one another. Indeed, I do not hesitate to aver that it is a more vital test than our orthodoxy. I am the last man in the world to say anything against orthodoxy, but I am here to say that it is not the final test. Orthodoxy is absolutely essential; this epistle has shown us that repeatedly, and it will show it to us again. We must believe the right things, for apart from that we have nothing at all and we have no standing whatsoever; so the correctness of belief is absolutely essential. And yet I say that when we come to the realm of experience and self-examination, the test of orthodoxy is not the ultimate test.

Alas, let us admit it, it is possible for a person to be absolutely correct and yet not to be a Christian. It is possible for men and women to give perfect intellectual assent to the propositions that are to be found in the Bible; it is possible for them to be interested in theology and to say that one theology is superior to another and to accept and defend and argue about it, and yet to be utterly devoid of the grace of the Lord Jesus Christ and of the love of God in their hearts. It is a terrible thought, it is a terrible possibility, but it is a fact. There have been men, also, who have clearly been perfectly orthodox—champions of the faith, and yet they have denied that very faith in the bitterness with which they have sometimes defended it. I repeat, the test of orthodoxy, while it is so vital and essential, is not enough.

There is something, as John shows us in these two verses without going any further, that goes very much more deeply and is a more certain guarantee of where we really are. I suggest that it is even a more thorough test than the exercise of faith as a principle. I need not emphasise that. Paul has done this once and for ever in 1 Corinthians 13 (here paraphrased): 'Though I have faith that I can remove mountains, and have not love, I am nothing. Though I speak with the tongues of men and of angels, though I have knowledge and understanding and wisdom, if it is without love, it is no good; it is like sounding brass or a tinkling cymbal—no use at all.' Faith is a most glorious and valuable thing, and yet there is something deeper than that. Indeed, there is a more thoroughgoing test, and it is this test of brotherly love—love for one another.

Likewise, this is a more thorough test than conduct and behaviour. John has a great deal to say about that; conduct and behaviour and deportment are of the most vital importance. 'Be not deceived,' says Paul. 'God is not mocked: for whatsoever a man soweth, that shall he also reap' (Gal 6:7). And remember what he tells the Corinthians: 'Be not deceived: neither fornicators, nor idolaters, nor adulterers, nor effeminate, nor abusers of themselves with mankind, nor thieves, nor covetous, nor drunkards, nor revilers, nor extortioners, shall inherit the kingdom of God' (1 Cor 6:9-10). Conduct is essential and all-important, and yet the fact that men and women live good, moral, and highly ethical lives does not prove that they are Christians. The ultimate test of our whole position is this question of love. Do we possess the love of which the Apostle is here speaking?

So let us approach it more directly. What is this love? Well, it is generally agreed that it has reference to Christian people. John is not talking about people who are not Christians; he is here emphasising this one thing to those who claim to be Christians, to those within the faith. And this, evidently, is an exhortation which is necessary. What does he mean when he exhorts and pleads with us to 'love one another'? I cannot think of a better way of putting it than simply to say that we are to be manifesting in our lives with one another, and in our attitude towards one another, everything that we read about love in 1 Corinthians 13. We are not to be puffed up; we are not to be easily provoked; we are not to think evil; we are not to rejoice in evil about others; we are to hope for all things and to hope for the best in other people.

I am afraid that as we read those words together, we all feel condemned. Loving one another is to love like that, and not only those whom we happen to like, but even those whom we dislike. That is the test of the Christian. You remember how our Lord put it in the Sermon on the Mount. He said, 'If ye love them which love you, what reward have ye?' (Matt 5:46). That is not difficult—anybody can do that—natural love does that. But the whole test of the Christian is to love the difficult person and to manifest 1 Corinthians 13 with the trying person.

'But I thought you said,' says someone, 'that this is only applicable to Christian brethren?' Yes, it is; but, alas, we all know that though we are Christians we are not perfect; there are things about all of us that irritate others. *God, forgive us for it.* There are things that should not belong to us, but they are there, and this calls for patience in others, it calls for sympathy, it calls for understanding; and that is what John is pleading for at this point. He is asking these people to do all they can to help one another, to bear with one another, not to be antagonistic, not to become irritated. If you see your brother at fault, be patient with him, pray for him, try to help him, be sorry for him, instead of feeling it is something that is hurting you. See it as something that is hurting him terribly and doing him great harm and robbing him of so much joy in his Christian life.

That is what love means—that you somehow detach yourself from the problem and do not think of it in terms of that which is hurting you, but look upon it as Christ did, and have compassion for that person, take hold of him, love him out of it. I do not want to go into this in detail because I am anxious rather to emphasise the great appeal which John makes and the terms in which he puts that appeal, trusting that as we do so we shall all not only feel condemned for our failure, but also that we shall feel a great sense of longing to live this Christian life in all its glory and in all its fullness.

Now John not only puts this as an appeal, he lifts it to a higher level. He goes further than that, and he puts it in such a way that it becomes something very solemn, and it becomes a warning. That, again, is something that is so typical and characteristic of the New Testament method of teaching holiness. It does not consist of a mere denunciation of sins or the doing of certain little things. It is so easy to stand and condemn people who do certain things; but that is not the teaching of holiness. *This* is holiness—loving one another—and this is to be seen in terms of our whole relationship to God. It is a great doctrinal matter, and the New Testament always puts the teaching about holiness in terms of ultimate doctrine. Let us see how John does this here.

He does it in a very characteristic way. John, as we have had occasion to see in our study of this epistle, had an interesting type of mind. There was a great deal of the poet and the mystic in him. His method is not logical like that of Paul. As someone has said, John thinks in circles; he generally starts on a practical point, then he philosophises about it in a Christian way, and then he arrives at some glorious statement of doctrine. And this is a perfect illustration of his method.

In my opinion, John ends with what Paul would have said at the start. John says, 'Beloved, let us love one another . . . every one that loveth is born of God.' Then comes the negative which he is so fond of: 'He that loveth not, knoweth not God,' and then he says, 'for God is love.' Now that is the poet's way of arriving at truth, but I think it will perhaps be more helpful to us, especially those of us who are not poetic and those of us who are more logically minded, if we put it the other way round. The fundamental statement is, 'God is love'; and because God is love, certain things must be true of us. That is the logical approach.

So, let us start like this, and more than ever do I feel my utter and complete inadequacy as I try to handle words like these. Indeed, who is sufficient for these things? What right has a pigmy man to make such statements as these? And yet it is true—'God is love.' No one can answer that; one trembles even to handle it; it cannot be analysed. I simply want to point out that John does not say merely that God loves us or that God is loving. He goes beyond that. He says, '"God is love"; God essentially is love; God's nature is love; you cannot think of God without love.'

Of course he has already told us that God is light in exactly the same way—that was the first pronouncement. 'This then is the message . . . God is light' (1:5), and in exactly the same way 'God is love' and God is spirit. This baffles the imagination; it is something that is altogether beyond our comprehension, and yet we start with it.

St. Augustine and others deduce from this the doctrine of the Trinity. I think there may be a great deal in that; this very fact that God is love declares the Trinity—God the Father loves the Son, and the link is the person of the Holy Spirit. Ah! this is high doctrine; it is beyond us. All I know is that God, in the very essence of His nature and being, is love, and you cannot think of God and must not think of Him except in terms of love. Everything that God is and does is coloured by this; all God's actions have this aspect of love in them and the aspect of light in the same way. That is how God always manifests Himself—light and love.

'Therefore, because that is the fundamental postulate, because that is so true of God,' John is saying, 'that works itself out for us like this: Because God is love, we ought to love one another, for three reasons.' The first is that 'love is of God'; in other words, love is from God, love flows from God. It is as if John were turning to these people and saying, 'You know, we ought to love one another. We ought more and more to clutch at the great privilege we have of being like God. God loves, and this love I am talking about,' says John, 'is something that only comes from God—it is derived from Him.'

John is not talking about natural love at all—let us get rid of that idea. The Greek scholars know that this is a word that really belongs to the New Testament. The pagans did not understand it; it was a new conception altogether. Indeed, there was a sense in which the Jews themselves did not understand it; it was something new that God gave to the world through Jesus Christ. Our whole idea of love is so debased, it is so carnal; it is the thing you read about in the newspapers or see in the cinema. But that is not the thing that John is speaking about. He is speaking about this love that comes from God, something that God Himself is doing. 'Beloved,' says John, 'love one another. Cannot you see that as you are doing this you are proving that you are of God? You are doing something that God Himself is doing.' How foolish we are not to rise to the great height of our calling; let us manifest the fact that we have received this from God. That is the first reason for brotherly love.

The second reason for loving one another is that it is the evidence of our new birth. 'Beloved, let us love one another: for love is of God; and every one that loveth is born of God.' Now that is why I said at the beginning that this is the most thorough test of whether we are true Christians or not. You see, what finally makes us Christians is that we are born again, we are born of God. It is not a certain intellectual proposition; it is not that we are defenders of the faith and so are concerned about being strictly orthodox; it is not that we are highly moral and ethical; it is not that we do a lot of good and are benevolent. The one thing that makes us Christians is that we are born of God, that we are partakers of the divine nature—nothing less than that, nothing short of that.

'Here is the thing that proves you are born of God,' says John in effect; and this works out in two ways. Only those who are born of God can love like this; nobody else can. The natural man cannot exercise this love; it is obvious that he cannot. Look at the life of the world and you see the breakdown; the natural man cannot love in this sense. The only people who can love as God loves are those who have received the nature of God. It is no use asking the world to 'love one another.' It is impossible; they are incapable of doing it. We need the divine nature within us before we can truly love one another. If within the church you have failure on the part of men and women to love one another, what hope is there for the world to do this? It is utterly impossible.

Let me put it like this: According to this argument, and this is the argument of the New Testament everywhere, those who are born of God must love one another—they cannot help it. If something of the divine nature is in me, and the divine nature is love—'God is love'—then there must be this principle of love within me. It must be here, it must be manifesting itself; and if I am not conscious of this life within me, and if I am not manifesting this life somehow or other, however feebly, then I am not a Christian.

As we have said, John does not put this merely as an exhortation. He puts it in such a way that it becomes a desperately serious matter, and I almost tremble as I proclaim this doctrine. There are people who are unloving, unkind, always criticising, whispering, backbiting, pleased when they hear something against another Christian. Oh, my heart grieves and bleeds for them as I think of them; they are pronouncing and proclaiming that they are not born of God. They are outside the life of God; and I repeat, there is no hope for such people unless they repent and turn to Him. They belong to the world; the murderous spirit of Cain is in them. God is love, and if I say I am born of God and the nature of God is in me, then there must be some of this love in me. 'Every one that loveth is born of God,' and everyone who is born of God loves—the two statements mean the same thing, so that this is proof positive, final evidence, of my new birth and that I am born of God.

Do you feel any love within you towards that person you naturally dislike, that person who is so irritating and can be in certain respects so hurtful to you? Do you know a sense of compassion and pity? Do you pray for that person? Can you truly say you are sorry? That is what love does. Do you feel that with regard to these people? If you are born of God, you must, however feebly.

And, lastly, John says that to love one another is evidence of spiritual knowledge. 'Beloved, let us love one another: for love is of God; and every one that loveth is born of God, and knoweth God.' He puts this negatively also: 'He that loveth not, knoweth not God.' In other words, it is by manifesting this life to one another that we give proof of the fact that we have a truly spiritual knowledge, that we really know God. Now this is the logical development of spiritual knowledge; it is to know God. God is love, and therefore the more I know God, the more will I know that God is love, and the more will I know about love.

We go through stages in this matter. Let us use Paul's analogy in 1 Corinthians 13. 'When I was a child, I spake as a child, I understood as a child.' Yes, but we are growing, says Paul in effect; '"now I know in part," but when I see Him face to face, I will know everything. I do not know everything now. I start with a little knowledge, but it is growing and developing as I walk in fellowship with God.' We start with knowing certain things about God: God is great, God is limitless in power, God is someone who is love and is prepared to forgive us for our sins. 'I know a whole series of things about God, and, you know,' says John in effect, 'as I go on and grow in Christ, I pay less and less attention to the things I know about God; now my interest is to know God Himself. I was interested in gifts, but I now want to know the Giver. My knowledge has become the knowledge of the person; and as my knowledge of the person increases, I know more and more that God is love. At the beginning there were times when I was tempted to doubt whether God loved me. Things went against me, and I felt I was not receiving a fair deal; but as I go on, I cease to think things like that. I know that God is love, and when I am tempted to question, I still say God is love. I know that more and more; and as I know more and more that God is love, I see that nothing matters but love. And the more I see this in God, the more I want to look at Him, and the more I love my brethren; and the more I love my brethren, the more I prove that God is love.'

This is a wonderful argument. I think that all writers on the spiritual life are agreed that the ultimate stage is this stage of loving. Knowledge and love become one at a certain point; knowing God means, I repeat, not knowing things *about* God but really knowing Him. The same word is used about God's knowledge of us. God said of the children of Israel through Amos, 'You only have I *known* of all the families of the earth' (Amos 3:2). He did not mean that He knew nothing about the others; He meant He knew them in this intimacy of love. Do we know that God is love, and are we giving proof of this by loving one another? It is not surprising that John exhorted us all to that. These are the reasons for loving one another.

But there is another point in exhorting men and women to love one another. You cannot command natural love, but you can command Christian love. This means that as I live with others, and as I am in this world of time, suddenly I may come across something that tempts me to act like the old, natural man. But as a Christian I am not to do that. Before I act, I am to say to myself, 'I am a Christian. I am born of God. I am unlike the natural man. I have no right to live like that. I must live as a new man. I will put off the old and put on the new. I will claim that God is in me, and the Holy Spirit, and that Christ dwells with me, and therefore I will not act like that; I must be like Him.'

In other words, you bring the Apostle's great argument to bear; you look upon that other person, and you see him with the eyes of God as it were. You have pity; you have compassion; you feel sorry for the other person; you remember that you have been commanded to love one another as Christians. You just remind yourself of the three mighty arguments—love is of God, it belongs to us who receive the divine nature, it is the inevitable corollary of knowing God. It means being like God Himself.

What a privilege and what a glorious honour that God calls

upon us to be like Himself! 'Be ye therefore perfect, even as your Father which is in heaven is perfect' (Matt 5:48); and that was said in the context of loving one another.

'Beloved, let us love one another: for love is of God; and every one that loveth is born of God, and knoweth God. He that loveth not, knoweth not God; for God is love.'

4

The Manifest Love of God

> In this was manifested the love of God toward us, because that God sent his only begotten Son into the world, that we might live through him. Herein is love, not that we loved God, but that he loved us, and sent his Son to be the propitiation for our sins.
>
> 1 JOHN 4:9–10

In these two verses the Apostle continues with the theme of the vital importance of brotherly love. We have seen that he considers this theme in terms of his great proposition that 'God is love'; it is from that base that his whole appeal to us to love one another arises. Now here he continues with this same subject, this vital importance of our loving one another, we who claim to be Christians; and John proceeds to deal with this by elaborating that fundamental postulate of his that 'God is love.' He has told us that God is essentially love—not only that God loves us and that God is loving, but that God's very nature is love. As God is light, so God is love; and His holy love is something that covers the whole of His life and His every activity.

But now the Apostle is anxious to remind us that God is actually manifesting that essential nature of His. He is love, but mercifully for us He has *'manifested'* that love, He has made it unmistakably plain and clear. So we can put John's immediate argument like this: 'If only you really understood this love, if only you knew something about it, then most of your problems and difficulties would immediately vanish.' So he proceeds to tell us something further about this great and wondrous and glorious love of God.

Surely we all must agree that this is something that is equally true of us. The more I study the New Testament and live the Christian life, the more convinced I am that our fundamental difficulty, our fundamental lack, is the lack of seeing the love of God. It is not so much our knowledge that is defective but our vision of the love of God. Thus our greatest object and endeavour should be to know Him better, and thus we will love Him more truly. Now John's object is to help these first Christians to whom he writes in just this way, because he is quite sure that once they love God, they will love one another.

That is something we find running right through the Bible; the second commandment follows the first. The first commandment is, 'Thou shalt love the Lord thy God with all thy heart, and with all thy soul, and with all thy mind. . . . And the second is like unto it, Thou shalt love thy neighbor as thyself' (Matt 22:37, 39). But you will never do the second until you have done the first; so we must start with the love of God.

Now in these two verses we have a sublime statement of this. You notice how reminiscent this is of John 3:16: 'God so loved the world, that he gave his only begotten Son, that whosoever believeth in him should not perish, but have everlasting life.' It is just a variation of that. It is a wonderful statement concerning the love of God, but at the same time it is a perfect summary of the gospel. Indeed, I want to go further and suggest to you that these two verses together are a perfect and complete synopsis of Christian theology. And I am particularly anxious to emphasise that last statement. You notice that John does not content himself with just saying that God is love; he does not leave it at that. John says that the love of God can only be understood in the light of certain vital truths, and those truths are highly theological.

Let me explain what I mean by that and give my reasons for putting it in that particular form. I think this is a statement that needs to be repeated and emphasised at the present time, because the great tendency in this present century has been to put up as antitheses the idea of God as a God of love on the one side, and theology or dogma or doctrine on the other. Now the average person has generally taken up such a position as follows: 'You know, I am not interested in your doctrine. Surely the great mistake the Church has made throughout the centuries is all this talk about dogma, all this doctrine of sin, and the doctrine of the Atonement, and this idea of justification and sanctification. Of course there are some people who may be interested in that kind of thing; they may enjoy reading and arguing about it, but as for myself,' says this man, 'there does not seem to be any truth in it; all I say is that God is love.' So he puts up this idea of God as love over and against all these doctrines which the Church has taught throughout the centuries.

Now that is something which must be faced and faced very frankly. Indeed, is it not true to say that men have not only put up this idea of God as love over the doctrines I have mentioned, but they have gone so far as to say that they are not interested in the doctrine of the person of Christ? 'The one thing that matters,' they say, 'is that God is love. Jesus of Nazareth was a great teacher, but when you talk about the doctrine of the Incarnation and the Virgin Birth—I am not interested in these refinements. All I know is that Jesus was a wonderful man, and He taught us that God is love.' So this idea of God as a God of love has been used as the argument of all arguments for denouncing doctrine and theology.

But all that, according to these two verses which we are considering here, and according to the whole of the New Testament, is an utter travesty of the Christian truth and position. According to these two verses, people who thus put up as opposites the idea of God as love and these basic, fundamental doctrines can, in the last analysis, know nothing whatsoever about the love of God. Is it not interesting to observe that it is John, whom people like to call the Apostle of love, who is the one who outlines the love of God in this particular way and manner? It is as typical of his Gospel as it is of this first epistle; it is John who explains the love of God in this highly doctrinal and theological form.

The vital question which we must ask ourselves is this: How do we know that God is a God of love? What is the basis of our knowledge? What is my ultimate sanction for saying I believe that God is a God of love? 'All I am interested in,' says the average man, 'is that God is a God of love and that He will forgive my sins.' But how do you know that He will forgive your sins? What right have you to say that you believe that God will do that? Oh, how easy it is to use these expressions; but let us stop and ask the question quite simply: What is my authority, and how do I know?

I suggest to you that there are only two ultimate answers to that: You are either basing it upon your own or somebody else's philosophical conception of God, or you are accepting in simplicity, and as they are, the very statements that are made in the Bible concerning God and His love. I do not think that it is at all difficult to prove that the average person, and especially the kind of person of whom I have been speaking, bases his whole idea of a God of love solely upon his own thoughts. He has no proof if he denies these facts and doctrines. He says that he believes what he says he believes, but he cannot prove it—he has nothing to substantiate it. He believes it, and he says that others have said it, and therefore it must be the case; but as to any final, ultimate proof, he has none.

Now the Bible itself actually does teach us that God has manifested Himself and His love in different ways. God has manifested His love in creation; the very act of creating the world at all must have been a manifestation of it, and this is seen in the order and arrangement which we see in the world. In the same way you can deduce the love of God from Providence. Certain things that happen are indications of it. Indeed, our Lord and Saviour Jesus Christ once put it like this: '[God] maketh his sun to rise on the evil and on the good, and sendeth rain on the just and on the unjust' (Matt 5:45). The love of God, then, is something which is manifested in God's providential care for and dealings with mankind.

But the great statement of the Bible from beginning to end, and especially the great statement of the New Testament, is that the love of God is only to be seen finally, and to be known truly, when you look at what God has done for us and in us in and through the Lord Jesus Christ. That is the great theme of the Bible. The Old Testament is a book that looks forward to the coming of Someone. It is God's gracious promise that a deliverer, the Messiah, is going to come; and in the New Testament you have an account of how He came and what He did.

This is something which is absolutely essential. The love of God can only be finally understood and appreciated in the Lord Jesus Christ. It is what God has done in Him and through Him that ultimately reveals it all. 'In this was manifested the love of God toward us, because that God sent his only begotten Son into the world, that we might live through him. Herein is love, not that we loved God, but that he loved us, and sent his Son to be the propitiation for our sins.' That is the manifestation of the love of God, says John, and here again is a compendium of theology, a synopsis of doctrine. There is no greater theological statement in the whole Bible than these two wonderful verses.

John does not say, 'God is love' and then pass on to something else. He says, 'If you want to know anything about love, you must realise these truths, because it is in this way that God has manifested His wondrous love to us. Apart from these things, you know nothing about love.' But let me go further. The love of God, I maintain, is only understood and felt in terms of theology, and to reject the theology is to reject the love of God and to be bemusing ourselves with some hypothetical and imaginary love. 'In this was manifested the love of God,' and here we have John's exposition of it.

Having, therefore, emphasised that fundamental attitude, let me attempt with reverence to look at this glorious and sublime statement. Would you like to join 'with all the saints,' as Paul puts it, in trying to measure and estimate 'the breadth, and length, and depth, and height; and to know the love of Christ, which passeth knowledge' (Eph 3:18-19)? This is how John proceeds. We are, of course, attempting the impossible. We are going to measure the immeasurable; we shall try to plumb the depths that no man can ever reach; we shall ascend the height which no man can ever aspire unto; and yet, says Paul, let us do it. And as we attempt to do so now, let us be guided by the Apostle John.

His general proposition is this: God's love has been manifested in what He has done for us or in us in the Lord Jesus Christ. So let us start in the depths; let us start to look at the love of God and attempt to measure it by looking at ourselves. You will never know the love of God until you know yourself. We will never appreciate the love of God until we know the startling truth about ourselves apart from Him and about His wondrous grace. God, we are told, has loved us. Why? Has God loved us because we are lovable? Has He loved us because we are such kind and wonderful people, so deserving of His favour?

Consider the answer of the Apostle John in these two verses: the love of God, let me emphasise it again, is only to be understood theologically. Here is what we are told: God sent His only begotten Son that we might live through Him; from which I deduce that apart from Him we are dead, and that is the fundamental statement about man as the result of sin which runs right through the Bible. 'You hath he quickened,' says Paul writing to the Ephesians, 'who were dead in trespasses and sins' (Eph 2:1). All of us, apart from Jesus Christ, are in a state of spiritual death. We not only lack a knowledge of God, we lack an understanding of spiritual things; the great spiritual faculty that God gave man at the beginning is lying dormant. As a result of sin we have no life in us; we do not *live*, we *exist*. Read the first three verses of Ephesians 2, and there you have it: 'And you hath he quickened, who were dead in trespasses and sins; wherein in time past ye walked according to the course of this world, according to the prince of the power of the air, the spirit that now worketh in the children of disobedience: among whom also we all had our conversation in times past in the lusts of our flesh, fulfilling the desires of the flesh and of the mind; and were by nature the children of wrath, even as others.' Dead—dead to God and to His spiritual qualities—dead to everything that is truly uplifting and ennobling—living according to the course of this life and of this age— an existence in a state of death. This is what John says—namely, that Christ came that we might live through Him; without Him we are dead.

But not only that. According to the Bible, far from being lovable and loving, men and women by nature hate God. 'Herein is love, not that we loved God'; that is, it is not the case that we in our natural state loved God and He responded to our love. The picture of the Bible is not that people are ever seeking for God because they love Him. That is the popular theology—that men and women are seeking God and that God responds to their request. Not at all! 'Not that we loved God, *but that he loved us*.' People, by nature, do not love God. According to the Bible, by nature and as the result of sin and the Fall, they are enemies of God. 'The carnal mind'—the natural man—'is enmity against God,' says Paul; 'it is not subject to the law of God, neither indeed can be' (Rom 8:7).

Is all that not the simple truth, and must we not all confess that by nature and apart from the light we have had in the gospel of Jesus Christ, when things go wrong the feeling is one of enmity? We are enemies, aliens, strangers, at enmity against God. 'God commendeth his love toward us, in that, while we were yet sinners. . . . For if when we were enemies, we were reconciled to God by the death of his Son . . .' (Rom 5:8, 10). That is the picture that is given of man; dead and hating God; far from loving him, but rather feeling opposed to Him; and because of all that, man by nature is under the wrath of God and deserves the punishment of God for his sins. That is Paul's statement, and it is the statement of the Bible everywhere.

We are, let me remind you, trying to measure this amazing love of God, and that is the first measurement: men and women down in the dregs and depths of sin, deserving nothing but wrath, and with nothing to be said for them. And the whole argument of the New Testament is that until we see that that is the simple truth about us, we do not begin to know anything about the love of God. That is the first step in measuring it.

But let us go on to the second. Let us proceed immediately from the depths right up to the heights. We have seen man. Now let us look at God and see what He has done, and the astounding thing we are told is that God has 'sent *His only begotten Son* into the world.' That is the central message of the New Testament, and indeed of the whole Bible; it is about a person called Jesus Christ of Nazareth. Who is He? John has been talking about Him; his whole message is about this person, and this is what he tells us about Him: He is God's 'only begotten Son.' The original reads like this: 'In this was manifested the love of God toward us, because that God sent his only begotten Son into the world, that we might live through him.' His Son–His only begotten Son. That statement means that this person has a unique kinship with God. It is John's way of saying that Jesus Christ is none other than the eternal Son of God, co-eternal, equal with God, dwelling in the bosom of God, the effulgence of God, one with God, the second person of the blessed Trinity.

But, you see, John puts this in another form: God '*sent*' His Son. So if Jesus Christ is someone who has been 'sent' into the world, he must have existed before. None of us have been sent into the world. We are born into this world, but here is someone who was sent from somewhere else. He existed before, in eternity. His birth at Bethlehem was not the beginning for Him. He began His earthly course, He came, He was sent from heaven. That is another way of estimating the love of God. God has manifested His love towards us in that He, there in glory, has sent from heaven, with its eternal bliss and absolute perfection, into this world His only begotten Son. We cannot fathom this—it escapes us. But can we try to imagine something of what this means. God, we are told, 'sent' His Son; He asked Him, His only begotten Son, to come into this world, consisting of men and women such as I have already been describing. 'In this was manifested the love of God,' that out of heaven He 'sent His only begotten Son,' the one who is in His own bosom.

Fathers and mothers, does this mean anything to you? Think of your own love to your children and multiply it by infinity, and that is God's Father-love to God the Son; and yet He sent Him into the world. So you know nothing about the love of God unless you believe the doctrine of the Incarnation. Believe me, you cannot talk of the love of God dwelling in you unless you know that Jesus of Nazareth is the unique and only begotten Son of God. If you are uncertain about the person of Christ, you have no love of God in you—you are fooling yourself. You must not put the love of God as an opposite to the doctrine of the person of Christ. He is the God-man; all the miracles and the supernatural power, all the fullness of the Godhead dwells in Him bodily. Understanding the person of Christ is absolutely essential to understanding the doctrine of the love of God.

But let us pause there. From the heights let us come down again to the depths, and let us glance for a moment at what the Lord Jesus Christ has done. We have said that God has 'sent His only begotten Son' from heaven; but He sent Him, John says, '*into the world.*' O blessed be His holy name! The Son, the only begotten Son, came into this world. We are measuring the love of God—and this is the way to measure it. Look at the world into which He came. You remember His birth and what we are told about it. This is the sort of world that the eternal Son of God, who had come from heaven, came into: There was no room for Him and for Mary and Joseph in the inn. The selfishness of mankind was such that even a woman in this condition did not get a room and had to go into a stable; so the Lord of glory was placed in a manger in a stable. That is the sort of world He came into; a selfish, grasping, self-centred world in which every man is out for himself.

You also remember the story of Herod and the massacre of the innocents—all the malice, envy, hatred, and bloodshed. And, oh, the poverty into which He came! They could not afford to give the price of the highest offering for Him; they had to offer the two turtledoves—they could not afford any more. He was born into a very poor home; he knew something of the squalor and the need that accompanies poverty. And for thirty years He lived a very ordinary life as a carpenter, mixing with ordinary people. Can you imagine what it must have meant to Him, the Lord of glory, the eternal Son of God who came out of God's eternal bosom, to see sin firsthand? To look at the ugliness of evil and sin and see it face to face? The shame of it all and the foulness of it all! We are measuring the love of God, and that is the measure of it. How could He in all His purity and holiness ever come from heaven and live for thirty years in the kind of world in which you and I are living? How could He have done it? How could He stand or bear it?

Then watch Him in His ministry, teaching His pure, loving, holy doctrine, seeing the opposition that arose. Look at the people looking at one another, asking their questions, trying to trip Him—the cleverness they display in trying to pull Him down. Look at the scheming; look at the treachery even among His own friends; look at Him deserted by all His disciples; look at Him on trial; look at the crown of thorns they put upon His holy brow—that is the world into which He came. 'In this was manifested the love of God . . . that God sent his only begotten Son into the world.'

But more, he sent Him, we are told, to be '*the propitiation for our sins.*' What does this mean? Here, of course, is the great classic doctrine of the atonement, and it means that he sent Him into this world in order that He might become the sin offering for us. It means that God 'hath made him to be sin for us, who knew no sin;

that we might be made the righteousness of God in him' (2 Cor 5:21). It means that Jesus Christ is not only the priest, but He is also the offering, the propitiation, the sacrifice offered. God sent Him into the world in order that God might punish our sins in Him. He has made His Son the sacrifice; it is a substitutionary offering for your sins and mine. That was why He was there in the Garden sweating drops of blood, because He knew what it involved—it involved a separation from the face of His Father. And that is why He cried out on the Cross, 'My God, my God, why hast thou forsaken me?' There we see the love of God not only in the world He came into, but in the propitiation, the sacrifice, the substitutionary death, so that you and I might be delivered. Herein was manifested the love of God, that God sent His only begotten Son to death, to the cruel shame and agony and suffering of the cross, to be made sin for us who Himself knew no sin and so was innocent.

But thank God, it did not stop at that. He raised Him again from the dead and thereby proclaimed that the sacrifice was enough, that the law was satisfied, and that everything was complete. I say again, you do not begin to know anything about the love of God until you see that if Christ had not died on the cross in that way, God could not forgive sin. I say it with reverence: that is God's way of making forgiveness, for without the doctrine of the atonement you do not understand the love of God. Let me beseech you, never again put the love of God and doctrine as opposites. It is only in this way you understand the love of God. There is the depth again.

But let us once more rise from the depths to the heights; let us rise with Him in resurrection, and let us look at what He has meant to us as the result of that. Christ died—that is what we are told; He has been made 'the propitiation for our sins.' In other words, as the result of what He has done, God forgives us for our sins; by His death we are reconciled to God in Him; we have redemption through His blood. The blood is essential; never speak about it as if it were something that is legalistic. 'In [Him] we have redemption through his blood, even the forgiveness of sins' (Col 1:14). In Him we are reconciled to God, pardoned, forgiven, and restored. Yes, and even more, God sent His Son into the world, that we might live through Him. We receive the gift of life; we begin to live, because He came. We are given His nature; we are given His power. He becomes One who resides in us; we live in Him, and He is in us; we live through Him. There we again rise to the height.

That is what God has done for us in His love through Christ—pardon, forgiveness, peace, reconciliation, life anew. We begin to live in a new world, and we see new possibilities. We know something of His mighty working in us and the power which operates in us. That is how the love of God is manifested, that He sent His Son, and the Son has taken hold of us and, as Paul puts it, has 'raised us up together, and made us sit together in heavenly places in Christ Jesus' (Eph 2:6). But shall we dare to venture to rise still higher and to the highest height of all?

Finally, why has God done all this? Why has God had anything to do with such creatures as men and women, dead in trespasses and sins, rebels—hating Him, being against Him, turning His world into a living hell? Why did God ever even look on them, let alone send His only begotten Son to them, and even to the cruel death and shame of the cross, making Him a sin offering? Why has God done this? What led Him to do it? What is this love of God, and wherein does it consist? 'Not that we loved God, *but that he loved us*,' moved by nothing but His own self-generated love. Though we are what we are, 'God is love,' and His great heart of love, in spite of all that is in us, unmoved by anything save itself, has done it all.

I do not know what your feeling is at this moment, but I will tell you what mine is. I cannot understand the hardness of my own heart. How could any of us look at all this and believe it and not be lost in love to God? How can we contemplate these things and not be utterly broken down? How can any hatred remain in us? How can we do anything but love one another as we contemplate such amazing love? How can we look at these things and believe them and not feel utterly unworthy and ashamed of ourselves and feel that we owe all and everything to Him and that our whole lives must be given to express our gratitude, our praise, and our thanksgiving? Oh, let us resolve together to meditate more and more every day upon this amazing love. Look at it in terms of yourself, in terms of God, what God has done, what Christ has done. Go over these things; study them; read the Bible about them; examine them. Go on looking at them; contemplate them until your heart is broken and you feel the love of God possessing you wholly. 'Love so amazing, so divine, demands my soul, my life, my all.'

5
We Ought Also . . .

Beloved, if God so loved us, we ought also to love one another.

1 JOHN 4:11

These are the words that follow in exalted magnificence the ones we were considering in verses 9 and 10, and this word 'so' in our text refers us back to those two great verses. Nothing sublimer than that can be found anywhere, and we have looked at those verses and tried through them to measure the breadth and the height and the depth of the love of God in Jesus Christ. We have considered that glorious revelation of the love of God, and now these are the words that follow. 'Beloved, if God so loved us, we ought also to love one another.'

I wonder how you felt as you read these words. I wonder whether there is anybody who feels that it is a bit of an anti-climax, after that magnificent contemplation of God's revelation of His love, to have an exhortation, an appeal, to love one another. I always feel myself that when we come to a verse like this, after verses like 9 and 10, we place ourselves in one of the most thorough and profound tests of our spiritual perception and understanding that we can ever face. I do not hesitate to say that it is a verse like this that really tests where we stand spiritually. Verses 9 and 10 are, of course, the essential doctrine; I described them as a synopsis of Christian theology because in them we see the doctrines of man, of sin, of the person of Christ, of the Trinity, of the Incarnation, of the atonement, the resurrection and the ascension. It is all there, and it is absolutely essential; but our test in this verse is equally essential, equally a part of the truth. It tests our spirituality in this sense: it shows whether we are deeply and vitally concerned about these things or whether we just look at truth in general.

This is another characteristic of the gospel—the New Testament message. Have you not noticed how often it does this sort of thing? It takes you to the heights and then suddenly brings you down to the plain. And that is the way, I think, in which we should approach this statement—with, first of all, a bit of self-examination. Is our first feeling as we hear it, 'Ah, well, there is not going to be anything very wonderful to consider here? We are really again just facing an exhortation and an appeal to love one another. It was marvelous to look at the manifestation of the love of God and to contemplate all those great doctrines. How glorious all that was, but, "You ought also to love one another"—this is going to be unpleasant!' I trust nobody is reacting like that, but a verse like this does test us; it finds out exactly where we are and places us in our spiritual condition.

There are two obvious answers to such an attitude which stand out on the surface of this statement. Let me put them like this: First and foremost, Christianity, the Christian gospel, is not merely truth to be contemplated. It is that, but it is also a life which is given and a life which is to be lived. Let me put that in terms of a comparison like this: Those two verses which we considered earlier and this verse which follows make me think instinctively of the records we have in the Gospels of what happened on the Mount of Transfiguration. Our Lord took Peter and James and John aside; they went up into the mountain together, and He was transfigured before them. Moses and Elijah appeared and began to speak, and the three disciples were lost in a sense of wonder and rapture. Peter, the spokesman, jumped in as usual and said, 'Let us make three tabernacles; one for thee, and one for Moses, and one for Elijah' (Mark 9:5), by which he meant, 'Let us stay here; this is magnificent, this is glorious, this is wonderful.' But in effect our Lord said, 'No, Peter, there are great and terrible problems at the foot of this mountain. There is a man coming even now with a lunatic boy who is helpless, and my disciples whom we left behind cannot deal with him. We have to go down; we cannot stay here and contemplate the glory; we must go down and do something in the plains.'

That is the sort of thing we have in our text here, and we had a similar feeling when we dealt with those verses at the beginning of Chapter 3.[1] We were certainly on the Mount in verses 9 and 10, beholding glorious things; but we must not stay there. Christianity, let me emphasise this again, is not merely a truth to be contemplated—it is a life which is given and a life which must be lived. Unless our contemplation of truth leads us to do something about our own lives and about other people, that contemplation is useless.

We are here, of course, face to face with the whole error of what is called mysticism; that, I think, is its carnal error. The mystic is very concerned about the love of God. He is right when he says that the *summum bonum*, the highest good, is the contemplation of the love of God and sets out upon the mystic way. He puts himself under very rigid discipline; he will deny himself many things which the world affords him, quite legitimate things in themselves, because he is hoping to arrive at this knowledge of love. But the tragedy of the mystic is that he does all that in a more or less philosophical manner. He is concerned simply to *contemplate* love, and the result is that he is far remote from love. He is a wonderful man himself, but he does not know anything about the problems of life and human existence. He does not help other men and women.

How different from the Lord Himself, the friend of publicans and sinners, the one who said to Peter, 'No, we must not build a tabernacle here and stay here; we must go down and do something about those problems which are down there.' Mysticism is, in a sense, the very antithesis of the New Testament teaching. Thank

God that, according to the New Testament, love is not a feeling only. It is not something even that you contemplate philosophically. Love is the most active and practical thing in the world, and it shows and manifests itself in action. 'In this was manifested the love of God toward us.' 'Beloved, if God so loved us, we ought also to love one another.' Never separate these two things; they belong together.

Then my second general remark, which is obvious on the very surface of the text, is that this statement is the characteristic New Testament method of teaching holiness. I suggest you will never find a more typical New Testament expression of the teaching of sanctification and holiness than you have in these verses. Let me put that negatively. I am prepared to prove the contention that the New Testament nowhere comes to us and says something like this: 'Wouldn't you like to have a further blessing—wouldn't you like to have an abundant life—wouldn't you like to be living life with a capital *L*—wouldn't you like to be living the victorious life? Now it is all here, and you only have to receive it.'

The New Testament never does that. Rather, it teaches holiness in the way it does it here. It does not say, 'You are missing a great deal; there is a wonderful, higher life possible to you.' No! It says, 'My friend, you are living a low type of Christian life, and you have no right to be doing so. You ought to be ashamed of yourself for doing so; you are denying the gospel you believe. "Beloved . . . you ought."' The New Testament pronounces this as a kind of divine logic. It says, 'You have no right to be living any other kind of life if you call yourself a Christian, if you say you believe all that.' That is the New Testament method.

Let me put it like this: The living of the Christian life, according to the New Testament, is not primarily dependent upon some experience or some blessing which we have received. It is, rather, the outworking of the truth which we claim to believe. Now I suggest that that can never be repeated too frequently. Go through these New Testament epistles, and I think you will always find that

that is their invariable method. The first half of most of these epistles is pure doctrine, a reminder to the people of what God has done to them and the exalted position in which they have been placed. And then the writer says, 'Therefore . . .'

I can never understand people's objection to logic. The New Testament is full of it. It is here—'If God so loved us . . . then you ought.' We talk about divine imperatives. Well, here, if you like, is one. If you believe, then it must follow on; you have no right to be in any other position. Everything in the New Testament is in terms of truth. You are not exhorted by the New Testament not to sin and to live a good life in order that you may live life with a capital *L*. Not at all! The New Testament tells you, 'Ye are not your own. For ye are bought with a price' (1 Cor 6:19-20); so you have no right to use the body for fornication.

I wonder why we object to the truth being put like that. Why do we prefer it to be put in some sentimental form? Why avoid this tremendous logic? This is the New Testament method. If I say I believe *this*, then I must live like *that*. There is no use in my saying I believe *this* unless I behave like *that*, and there are terrible warnings against not doing this. The New Testament teaching of holiness is always in terms of truth. It is something that is to be applied; so let us proceed to do so, let us work this out together. I grant you that this is not a pleasant procedure; I grant you that it is much nicer to look at verses 9 and 10. It is even easier for the preacher!

John writes this epistle in order that these people may conquer the world in which they are living. He says, 'I write unto you, that your joy may be full'; and he goes on to say, in effect, 'If you want your joy to be full, you must put the Christian belief into practice.' We are engaged in Christian warfare; we believe in the fight of faith; and here is the way to learn how to fight it. Let us now get down to practicalities.

I am a Christian in this world, and there are other Christians. We are members of churches together, and I find some of these people to be rather difficult. I find that there are Christians whom I do not like by nature and instinctively. That was the position in the early church, and it is still the same; that is why John is making this great appeal. 'Beloved, let us love one another: for love is of God.' The whole of this section, from verse 7 right on to the first verse of the next chapter, is all about the question of brotherly love, and here he tells us how to do this. Now the question is, what do you do about it when you come up against these other people who seem to irritate you and are a problem to you and who really are making things rather difficult?

Here is John's answer: 'If God so loved us, we ought also to love one another.' This means something like this: Instead of giving way to that instinctive feeling that I have, instead of speaking or acting or reacting at once, I stop and I talk to myself. I remind myself of the Christian truth which I believe, and I apply it to the whole situation. Now that is something which you and I have to do. This life of which the New Testament speaks, as I am never tired of pointing out, is full of the intellectual aspect. It is not a feeling. You do not wait until you feel like loving other people—you make yourself love other people (*'we ought'*). According to the New Testament, Christians can make themselves love other Christians, and they are failing sadly if they do not do so.

How do they do it? They remind themselves of this truth: 'If God so loved us.' In other words, this is the procedure. The first thing I do when I feel irritated and disturbed and bewildered and perhaps antagonistic is to look at myself. Now that is half the battle. We all know perfectly well from experience that in this kind of problem the whole difficulty is that we are always looking at the other person and never at ourselves. But if I start with myself—if God so loved *me*—what do I find?

But usually I instinctively feel that I am being wronged, that I am not being dealt with fairly. I feel it is the other person who is difficult, and if only this other person could somehow change, there would be no difficulty, and all would be well and we should live happily together. 'One minute!' says the gospel; 'stop for a moment and look at yourself and remind yourself of exactly what you are.' The gospel brings us immediately face to face with this self that is in us which is the cause of all these troubles. 'In this was manifested the love of God toward us, because that God sent his only begotten Son into the world, that we might live through him . . . he loved us, and sent his Son to be the propitiation for our sins.'

In other words, let me remind you again of the truth we have been considering, that by nature we are dead in trespasses and sin, and that as Christians the old man and the old nature are still there. And the old man and the old nature can be described in a word: *self*. Self causes all these troubles. Self-will, self-love, self-trust, self-exaltation—these are the troubles. When we are honest with ourselves and examine ourselves, I think we will find that most of our troubles and difficulties arise from these causes. Let me give you a list which I have read in a book of the manifestation of this self-love. This is how it manifests itself: self-centredness, self-assertion, self-conceit, self-indulgence, self-pleasing, self-seeking, self-pity, self-sensitiveness, self-defence, self-sufficiency, self-consciousness, self-righteousness, self-glorying.

Is there anyone who would like to say that this is not a true description of himself or herself? That is the sort of persons we—all of us—are. It is no use denying it; that is the effect of the fall and of sin; that is what it has made of us. Self-centredness—looking at myself, watching myself, examining myself, always regarding myself. Self-assertion—asserting myself; I desire things, and I must have them. Self-conceit—how ready I am to defend myself and to condemn the same things in others! Self-indulgence—I am very indulgent with myself; I prohibit things in the other person, but it does not matter if I do the same thing myself. Self-pleasing—always doing things that please *me*. Self-seeking—always out for self. Self-pity—why should people treat me like this?—I have done no harm; I am not in the wrong at all—why should people be so difficult?—I am having a hard time and it really isn't fair. Self-sensitiveness—how touchy I am, how easily wounded, imagining difficulties and attacks, seeing them when they are not there, an abominable sensitivity. Self-defence—always on the defensive, waiting for people to be unpleasant, and because we are like that, we almost make them unpleasant—we are on the defensive.

Self-sufficiency, self-consciousness—oh, to get away from self! 'O wretched man that I am! who shall deliver me from the body of this death?' (Rom 7:24). How can I get away from this wretched, ugly self I am always thinking about? Isn't that the cry of every man and woman convicted of sin by the Holy Ghost? Now the effect of verses 9 and 10 is to expose all that, and I really am not prepared to listen to people who tell me that they glory in the revelation of God's love unless they have dealt with themselves. There is no value in any such striving to keep the tenets of the Christian faith unless they have made you see yourself in the world, unless it has flashed upon you in such a way as to make you see this manifestation of self; that is what the love of God always does. 'Herein is love, not that we loved God, but that he loved us'; incredible, that God could love such a person as I have been describing. That is the amazing thing! That is love, says John.

Therefore, if you believe and know all that, it makes you see yourself as you are, and do you see what happens at once? The moment you see yourself like that, you cry with John Bunyan when he says:

He that is down need fear no fall,
He that is low no pride.

John Bunyan meant that when I see myself as I really am, nobody can insult me. It is impossible, because they can never say anything that is bad enough about me. Whatever the world may say about me, when I know myself, I know that they do not know the truth about me—it is much worse than they think. When we really see ourselves in the light of this glorious gospel, no one can hurt us, no one can offend us. We see ourselves in the dust, and we are so low that no one can send us lower. 'Beloved,' says John, '*if*

God so loved us . . .' You must start with yourself. Before you begin to defend yourself against that other person who you think is offensive or who has acted in an offensive manner, look at yourself and see yourself, and when you have seen yourself, you will be 75 percent of the way towards solving the problem.

But we do not stop there. Having seen ourselves, of course, we then go on to look at others. 'If God so loved us, we ought also to love one another.' Now you are looking at the other person, but of course you are doing so having first of all seen yourself. What a difference that makes! When you are lifted above another person, you look down upon them; but when you are groveling in the dust, you of necessity have to look up at that other person, and the condition is different at once, the perspective is different.

Let me summarise this. When the love of God is operating in our hearts, when we believe this gospel and reason out the meaning of this love, what happens is that we see the person rather than the thing that the person is doing. And is that not half the trouble in these human relationships? We see what people are *doing*—we do not see *them*. Now the gospel makes us see them as souls, objectively, and not only in terms of actions or in terms of what they are doing to us.

Still more specifically, let us put it as follows: When I look at these matters in the light of the glorious revelation of God's love, I see myself. Then I look at this other person who is making things difficult for me—as I thought at first—and this is what I see: I do not really see the offensive action of the person; I see a victim of sin, a victim of Satan. The gospel enables me to differentiate between the actions of that person and the person behind them.

That is exactly what God did with us when He loved us in Christ. God looked down from heaven and saw us on earth and saw our miserable actions. How could God ever love a sinner? Well, the answer, of course, is that God differentiates between the sinner and the sin. God loves the person and the soul in spite of the action. God draws that vital distinction, and He has pity upon us. He is sorry for us; He does not stop merely to look at what we do.

He says, 'There is a soul I want to save.' He draws that distinction, and when you and I are animated by the love of God, we do exactly the same thing. This love of God enables us to look at the people who may be offensive to us and to feel sorry for them. We will say about them, 'Poor things; they are just victims of sin and Satan, and they do not know it. It is the god of this world who has them in his grip; it is this foul canker that is in them—*that* is the trouble.'

Think of a man with terrible sores. You love that person. Now, because he has these terrible sores, do you hate him? No; you love the person in spite of the offensive sores on his skin. And we must do the same thing about the sinner. We must see the soul at the back of it all; we must see men and women conforming to sin and Satan like ourselves, and when we do that we begin to feel sorry for them. As God has had pity upon us, we find ourselves praying for them. We say, 'God, have mercy upon them. We know it is Satan and sin in them; manifest Thyself to them, and make them glorious children of God.' That is how it works. 'If God so loved us, we ought also to love one another.'

And the third step is that we now see ourselves and the other person as joint-sharers in salvation, as joint-heirs of the same glory awaiting us, and what a wonderful thing that is! Instead of looking at them as possible enemies, I see them as men and women who were one with me in sin, but who are now one with me in the great salvation that God has sent in the person of His Son. We see one another as pilgrims traveling together towards the same country, and by the eye of faith we look into it and we say, 'I am going to heaven, and so is that person; we are going to be there together.' How can we then look at the face of God and remember we hated one another on earth? We cannot do it; we are fellow-pilgrims, joint-heirs with Christ, children of the same Father, going to the same Home. How ridiculous it is to be at variance; we must become one—we must love that person. We see ourselves, thus, in the light of the glorious gospel.

And then, lastly, the contemplation of this truth makes us

realise what we owe to the love of God ourselves, and that therefore we must be the same towards others.

In the parable in Matthew 18 (vv 23-35), our blessed Lord Himself put this truth perfectly. He said that there was once a king who took a reckoning with his servants, and he found one who owed him the great sum of ten thousand talents. The poor man had nothing wherewith to pay this debt, so the lord commanded that he should be put into prison with his wife and children. But the servant went on his knees and begged the lord to have mercy upon him. He said in effect, 'Give me time, and I will pay you everything.' So the lord forgave him everything, and the man went out. But then he found a man who owed him one hundred pence, and he said to him, 'Pay me what you owe me.' The poor man replied, 'I cannot, but have patience with me and I will pay you all.' The man said to him, 'You must pay it all now,' and he had him cast into prison. But when the lord was informed of this, he condemned this unrighteous servant and cast him into prison. Do you remember our Lord's words at the end? He said, 'Likewise shall my heavenly Father do also unto you, if ye from your hearts forgive not every one his brother their trespasses.' These are our Lord's own words; our Lord Himself makes the truth perfectly plain.

In a sense we say the same thing every time we say the Lord's Prayer together: 'Forgive us our debts, as we forgive our debtors.' But I wonder whether we catch the full meaning of the parable. The first servant owed his lord ten thousand talents, which comes to two million pounds. The first servant owed his lord all that money, and he was forgiven it all; but he refused to forgive his fellow servant for a much lesser amount. His debt was about four hundred thousand times more than the debt of the man whom he refused to forgive. That is our Lord's own picture, which being interpreted is this: My debt to God is infinite. If He forgives me the two million, how can I possibly refuse to forgive someone else for so much less?

Indeed, our Lord goes further and says that men and women who know they have been forgiven for so much must forgive others. They cannot help themselves. Those who know they are debtors to mercy alone, those who realise what God's love has done for them, cannot help forgiving. The love of God has so broken them that they feel they must; God has done so much for them, they must do the same for others. 'Beloved, if God so loved us, we ought also to love one another.'

You see, the love of God is active. God did not merely look in love upon us—He did something about it. He sent His only begotten Son. 'God so loved' that He sent Christ to the cross; He sent Him to the grave. This is not love in contemplation, but love in mighty action. God did something about it and thereby saved us. We ought so to love one another. I must do something about that difficult person. I must pray for him and help him; I must do my utmost to enable him to overcome his sin. I do not just condemn such people and say they are impossible—I must do my utmost to help them. God did that for me. He spared not His only Son, His only begotten Son. That is love; it means going out myself to do something as God did it. And if the love of God is in us, this 'ought' will come into operation. This is a divine imperative; we will love one another even as, and because, God has so loved us.

Beloved friend, I ask you again, have you seen yourself? Well, if you have, you see yourself as utterly undeserving of the least of God's mercies. All your self-righteousness has vanished and gone. And as you see yourself like that, you see that others are also victims of the same horrible thing which we call sin. So you are sorry for them and have pity upon them, and you do everything you can to help emancipate them, so that they may become sharers with you of the love of God. You do that so that you may march together through Emmanuel's land to the glory that remains, where there will be no sin, no sorrow, no sighing, no weeping, no tears—nothing at all to mar the perfection and the glory of this life of love. Let us then be up and doing. 'If God so loved us, we ought also to love one another.'

6
God Dwells in Us

> No man hath seen God at any time. If we love one another, God dwelleth in us, and his love is perfected in us.
>
> 1 JOHN 4:12

As we come to a consideration of this particular verse, I do not hesitate to say that in many respects it is, from the standpoint of exposition, one of the most interesting and, I would say, the most difficult of all the verses which we have hitherto considered in this epistle. Not that the truth which it contains is inherently more difficult or obtuse than many which we have already encountered, but from the standpoint of precise interpretation, it does present us with a problem. Those who are familiar with the commentaries on this epistle will know how this has always been so, the problem being, of course, exactly where to fit it in, and how to fit it in with its own context and to discover exactly what it was that the Apostle was anxious to convey on this particular point. That, perhaps, may very well lead us to say something which will be of interest and value to those who are students of the Bible. There is surely no interest and no occupation which can be more interesting and fascinating than to deal with a situation like this which confronts us as we come to expound such a statement, and for myself I feel that the only thing to do with a verse like this is to ask it questions.

And there we come upon a general principle that is always of great value in the exposition of Scripture. I feel that oftentimes we fail to expound correctly and we misinterpret Scripture because we do not talk to it and ask it questions. It is a very good and a very rewarding thing to do that with Scripture. Let me put it as simply as this: You get a verse like this, and you say to it, 'Well, why do you say that? Why do you say it in this way, and why do you say it just here?' In other words, no statement in Scripture is made in a haphazard manner, and we must never allow ourselves just to pass over a statement which seems to us to be suddenly interpolated without any connection or sense or meaning. That is never true of Scripture; if we can but arrive at its meaning, there is always some reason for what is being said, there is some link, there was some process in the mind of the writer, under the influence of the Holy Spirit, that led him at that particular point to say that particular thing. So I am suggesting that the way to arrive at that is to ask these questions—to put up possibilities and to consider them and to reject them one by one until you are left with an explanation which seems to you to be satisfactory, or the most satisfactory in the given situation. And that, inevitably, has to be done with this verse that we are now considering.

So why does John suddenly, in the midst of this argument, say, 'No man hath seen God at any time'? What is the connection? What does he mean? What was it that suddenly, at this point, made him burst out, as it were, with this extraordinary statement? Several answers have been put forward to those particular questions. There are those who would say that what John was really saying was something like this: Following on from verse 11, 'Beloved, if God so loved us, we ought also to love one another,' he then said, 'No man hath seen God at any time.' 'In other words,' John said in effect, 'the only way in which we can love God is by loving one another. We cannot see God, but we do see one another, and therefore the only way to love God is to love one another.' That is a possible and, in a sense, a plausible answer. It is as if John were saying to them, 'Get right out of your minds all this mystical conception of love. Finish with any such thought, and realise that there is no value in your saying that you love God unless you love your brother. You do not see God, but you do see your brother; so love your brother, and you are thereby loving God.'

There are others who would say that we ought to interpret it in this way: our love ought to be like the love of God itself, and the love of God, as John has just reminded us, is something which manifests itself in the realm of the concrete and the actual. 'God is love,' said John in effect, 'and God has manifested this love in that He has sent His only begotten Son into the world, that we might live through Him.' In other words, to love is not something sentimental or mystical, because love manifests itself by loving persons in the concrete. And John is saying to us, 'You must do something. No man has seen God at any time, and therefore if you want to claim that you are loving God, then love as God loves—love the people you see—love the brethren. This is the only real way in which you can love.'

Now those are the two most common explanations that are put forward as an attempt to expound to us why John suddenly introduced this idea of the invisibility of God, and yet it seems to me that we must reject both these suggestions at once. And I would argue that verses 19-21 in this very chapter we are considering make it imperative that we should reject them, because John says there that we love Him—namely, God—because He first loved us. 'If a man say, I love God, and hateth his brother, he is a liar: for he that loveth not his brother whom he hath seen, how can he love God whom he hath not seen?' (v 20). We shall give a detailed exposition of that later, but for the time being it is enough to establish this point. John does not say that we cannot love God except through loving our brethren; that is not his argument. Nor does he say that we can only love God by means of loving our brethren. Rather, he tells us that we are to love God—that we *can* love God and that we *should* love Him.

Take again our Lord's exposition of the great commandment: 'Thou shalt love the Lord thy God with all thy heart, and with all thy soul, and with all thy mind. . . . And the second is like unto it, Thou shalt love thy neighbor as thyself' (Matt 22:37, 39). So we must be very careful always not to put the second before the first, as these expositors would do. The first is to love God and then secondly to love our neighbour; we must never put the love of our neighbour before the love of God Himself.

But if we reject these two possible explanations, what is our explanation of the sudden introduction of this statement at this point? It seems to me that the explanation must be something like this: John is here introducing a new theme, a new subsidiary, a new idea, into his great discussion of this question of loving the brethren. And this new theme I would describe as the theme of the assurance of salvation; it is the whole question of our knowledge of God and of the way in which we can know God. In other words, I am suggesting that John here is linking up with that with which he left off at the end of verse 8. Let me reconstruct it to you in this way: 'Beloved,' he says, 'let us love one another: for love is of God; and every one that loveth is born of God, and knoweth God. He that loveth not, knoweth not God; for God is love. . . . No man hath seen God at any time. If we love one another, God dwelleth in us, and his love is perfected in us.'

Now I am not suggesting by putting it like that that verses 9-11 are a digression. They are not, but they are, as it were, an amplification of that statement that 'God is love.' So we can put the argument in this way: The central theme of this whole section is the importance of loving the brethren. Why is that important? Here are John's arguments: The first is that 'love is of God,' it is a very wonderful thing, and therefore it is something we can covet, something that links us up with God and makes us God-like. Not only that, it is proof of the fact that we are born of God, and there again is something of vital importance. Every person who is born of God must love, for surely it is the only way we can demonstrate that we do appreciate the love of God to us. That was the argument of verse 11–'If God so loved us, we ought also to love one another.'

'But,' says John in effect, 'it is not only that, but it is important that you love the brethren from the standpoint of your own assurance of salvation and from the standpoint of your fellowship with God.' Now, verses 9-11 are just an amplification of the statement that 'God is love.' John says, 'In this was manifested the love of God toward us'; one of the ways in which we know that 'God is love' is what He has done in and through our Lord and Saviour, Jesus Christ. But having said that, having implied that, he goes back again to the main argument, which goes on from verse 12 to the end of the first verse of the next chapter. So the theme at this point is assurance of salvation and the importance of the love of the brethren in this matter of assurance, in this whole question of our knowledge of God and especially our knowledge of God as a God of love.

I think we have been dealing with what I would call the mechanics of this particular chapter, and it is of vital importance that we should do so. Though John has this peculiar style on which we have previously commented, though he thinks more like a poet than a logician, though he tends to arrive at his position in circles instead of straight lines, though there is something of the mystic in his thinking, nevertheless there is firm logic at the back of it; there is a definite line of reason. He does not throw out thoughts suddenly–there is an intimate connection between them all; and I suggest that if you bear this in mind, it will be helpful in understanding the remainder of the chapter.

So we look at it as follows: Let me use the comparison, if I may venture to do so, of a symphony. You have in these epistles movements, in exactly the same way as you have them in a symphony. We have often underlined and emphasised the various major movements of this epistle, but as you realise, within every movement in a symphony there is a further analysis, a sub-division. There are subsidiary themes even in the movement, and I suggest that that is what we are dealing with at this particular point. The particular movement here is *loving the brethren*; that is the ultimate idea, and John deals with it in an analytical manner. As I have reminded you, he says that this is very important for us because it is of God—there is the subsidiary idea in the movement. He says it is important also because we are born of God, and *those who are born of God must love*—there is another little theme. And then he says that this is tremendously important from the standpoint of knowing God.

Those who are interested in music—in Beethoven's music, for example—will realise how typical that is of a composer like Beethoven. Beethoven produces his movement; then a thought comes and he mentions it; and then he springs something else on us and says, 'This is what I am going to explain.' But all the time it is subsidiary to the main idea of the movement. I am suggesting that is what we have here. The main movement is concerned with the importance of loving the brethren, but then there are the subsidiary ideas, and the one he is going to explain and elaborate is this whole question of the knowledge of God, fellowship with Him, the assurance of salvation. That is what John really is ultimately concerned about in the whole epistle, as we saw at the beginning.[1] That is the astounding thing. 'Our fellowship is with the Father, and with his Son Jesus Christ' (1:3), and 'I am writing to you,' he says in effect, 'that you may enter into this fellowship. And now,' he says, 'if you really want to do that and to know how it can be done, there is nothing more important than that you should love one another, that you should love the brethren. This is vital in this whole question of knowing and having fellowship with Him.' So if we just bear that analysis in mind, I think it will help us to understand the whole situation.

Let us see, then, how John proceeds to handle this question: How can we arrive at this knowledge of God? That, surely, ought to be the great question in all our minds. 'Every one that loveth,' we are told, 'is born of God, and knoweth God. He that loveth not, knoweth not God; for God is love.' So how can we know God? How can we be sure of it? Do we not all understand the feelings in the mind and heart of Thomas and Philip as they are recorded in John 14: 'We know not whither thou goest; and how can we know the way?' 'You are telling us,' says Thomas in effect, 'that You are going to the Father. You talk about another world and about great mansions, and You tell us that you are going to prepare places for us. But You know, we do not understand this. Don't You realise that You are essentially different? We are of the earth, earthy; it is all vague, and we cannot grasp it. What is all this—how can we know?' And then Philip put the same question again: 'Seeing You are talking to us about the Father,' he said in effect, 'if only we could see the Father, it would be enough for us' (vv 5, 8).

That is the kind of craving and longing that is in the hearts and minds of all who are concerned about these things, this longing to know God for certain. You see it in the hymns:

Tell me Thou art mine, O Saviour,
Grant me an assurance clear.

William Williams
(trans. R. Lewis)

There is in the human heart undoubtedly a craving for certainty. We need not delay over this; the explanation of it is perfectly obvious. Our world is so uncertain—'Change and decay in all around I see.' Nothing is durable, nothing is steadfast; the things that can be shaken are being shaken. The whole world and the whole of life is so uncertain that there is nothing, in a sense, so deep in the human heart as a longing for stability, a certainty, an assurance, and this is something that has always manifested itself in the realm of religion. I use the term *religion* advisedly, for in every religion there is this craving for certainty, and it comes into practise even in the Christian faith, this longing for assurance. And the great question is, how is this to be obtained?

Indeed, another great theme is this: What is the nature of religious certainty? What is the character of religious knowledge? What is to happen to us as Christian people? On what, ultimately, is our assurance established? And John, in the verses that follow this twelfth verse, takes up that theme and gives us some answers to the question.

Let us look now at the answer given in this particular verse. First he makes a negative statement: our assurance or knowledge is not based upon external events. 'No man hath seen God at any time.' The first thing we must get rid of is any idea that there can be an immediacy of knowledge; we must once and for ever get rid of everything which would encourage us to think that through various stages we come to a literal vision of God.

This is a wonderful statement of Scripture which you find repeated on many occasions. You get the same words in John's Gospel: 'No man hath seen God at any time' (John 1:18). Then the Apostle Paul, in writing to Timothy, makes a very similar statement: '[God] only hath immortality . . . whom no man hath seen, nor can see' (1 Tim 6:16). This is a very important theme from the standpoint of a true understanding of our relationship with God.

There is a sense, perhaps, in which the Old Testament throws an almost clearer light upon this matter than the New Testament itself does, because in it we have a number of instances which are described as *theophanies*. A theophany means an appearance of God which was given to certain people. Consider, for example, the appearance that was given to Abraham, and also to Lot, and there are other examples of the same thing. These people saw and yet they did not see God, and they talk and write about 'the angel of the Lord.' Now there can be very little doubt that all those incidents were concerned with appearances of our Lord Jesus Christ before the Incarnation. He appeared temporarily in human form for certain specific purposes, and so we can still say that no man has seen God at any time.

But perhaps the most interesting example of all is what happened in the case of Moses. God said to Moses on one very special occasion, in effect, 'I will pass before you, I will appear unto you.' Yet observe what he also said. He said that Moses would be allowed to see His back, as it were. We are not told that Moses saw the face of God; but there was an appearance, God passing by, and Moses looked at His back (Exod 33:19-23). That is one of the most extraordinary scenes in the whole of the Bible, and yet obviously it is a situation which we must look at very carefully because it maintains this Biblical statement that 'no man hath seen God at any time.'

Of course, those very words that were used by our Lord in reply to Philip's question were the same thing in a different way. 'Show us the Father, and it sufficeth us,' said Philip; in effect he was saying, 'Give us a clear vision of the Father, and we will be content to go on even though you are leaving us.' 'Have I been so long time with you, and yet hast thou not known me, Philip? he that hath seen me hath seen the Father,' replied our Lord (John 14:8-9). 'It is not,' he said in effect, 'that you have seen the Father directly, with the naked eye; but look at Me and you will get your only conception of what the Father is like.' Is that the Father? No, that is the Son; but the Father is in the Son, and the Son is in the Father; and the only way in which we can see the Father, so far, is to see the Son. In other words, we must still hold to this basic idea that no man has seen God at any time.

Now we cannot go into this matter in as great detail as we should like, but let me sum it all up by putting it like this: We must turn our back very resolutely upon every teaching which would ever lead us to try to obtain a direct vision of God. We should never covet visions; we should never try to come into that immediate vision of God. There is an ultimate promise given to us, thank God: 'Blessed are the pure in heart: for they shall see God' (Matt 5:8); that is the ultimate. There is a time coming, a day coming, when we shall see Him, but not yet; and while we are here on earth and in this earthly pilgrimage, we must not even desire it. We must not desire ever to hear audible voices or to have such visions as will give us a kind of mechanical, material security. There were many mystics who went in for that kind of thing and who claimed to have visions, and it seems to me that if we do set our minds upon things like that, we probably shall be seeing things. But the whole question that arises is, what do we see? You enter into the realm of hallucinations and the realm of psychology, not to say the realm of the psychic, and that is something that John was anxious to warn people against.

In those early centuries there were mysteries of religions—a peculiar mixture of mystery religions, great philosophies, and so on. Some people did not like the idea of faith; they did not like the life in which, as Paul describes it, 'We walk by faith, not by sight' (2 Cor 5:7). They wanted to see and hear, they wanted something tangible; and so they fasted, and they passed through certain rites. They had the appropriate music, and they brought in the artistic; everything was being done to get this vision, this immediacy, this directness. And the result was that they became victims of aberrations, of heresies, and of hallucinations. In addition to that, they thus lost this fundamental understanding of the utter inscrutability of God because of His utter holiness. Their moral life degenerated, and you have all the manifestations which invariably accompany this craving for the immediate. You see this today in connection with spiritism, those people who claim to see and hear—I am speaking generally; and John's great concern was to warn these people against that. Your assurance, he says, will not be based on visions or audible voices; it has to be based on something deeper and stronger.

On what, then, is it based? How can I know God? Well, in verses 9-11 John has partly answered that question. I know that God is love, in that He has manifested this in everything that has happened in the Lord Jesus Christ. I do not need a vision. God in

GOD DWELLS IN US 85

His grace may give me a vision, but I do not seek and covet one. Why? I have the facts of the Lord Jesus Christ; I have something concrete and tangible in the realm of history; God is there manifesting Himself as love.

But that is not all. I have something further, and it is this: God dwells in us. That is the second ground of my assurance, my certainty. 'No man hath seen God at any time.' Very well, then, do we go on in doubt and almost in despair wondering whether there is a God? 'No!' says John; 'if we love one another "God dwelleth in us, and his love is perfected in us."' Now, I confess very readily that I approach a theme like this with fear and with a sense of awe. Consider the great statement in John 14 of this intimate union between the believer and God the Father and God the Son, of their abiding in us and dwelling in us. We are familiar with chapters 14, 15, 16 and 17 of John's Gospel,[2] and here we have the same thing again. 'God dwelleth in us, and his love is perfected in us.' And John goes on to say (v 13), 'Hereby we know we that we dwell in him, and he in us, because he hath given us of his Spirit'; and in verse 15, 'Whosoever shall confess that Jesus is the Son of God, God dwelleth in him, and he in God.'

At this point, like Moses, we take off our shoes! We are concerned with something that is glorious and magnificent, and so we have to be very careful as we handle it. We are not discussing some people who lived in the first century; we are talking about ourselves. The statement is that if we love one another, God–God who is love, God the Almighty, God the eternal–*dwells in us*. What does this mean? Well, I think that the great thing at this point is to realise that we must not materialise that conception; that is always the danger here, to think of it in material terms. We can avoid that if we remember that other fundamental postulate of the Bible that God is spirit. We are using words that in a sense elude us, and yet that is the nearest we can get to this exalted conception. We must not think of God in material terms; God is spirit. It is God, who is spirit, who dwells in us.

Perhaps an illustration will help us here. In all of us there is what we call the soul, but what is the soul? A famous doctor once said that having dissected many human bodies he had never come across an organ described as 'the soul'—thereby, of course, betraying a pathetic ignorance of the spiritual definition of the soul. The soul is immaterial; it is not a substance, nor is it an organ; and no man dissecting the human frame should ever seek for it. The soul is a spiritual entity and quality. But I say that my soul is in me and that my soul will go out of my body.

I cannot get nearer to this conception than that, and as this which we call 'soul' is in our bodies, so we are told in Scripture that God who is spirit dwells in us; He takes up His abode in us and lives in us. It is not that the eternal God is resident in me in a peculiar sense. No; but in some strange manner God, the eternal God who is spirit, enters into my life, moves in my life, deals with my life, organises my life, and manifests Himself in my life. This is something we will never understand truly while we are in the body and in this world and life. It is in a sense comparable to the whole mystery of the Incarnation; the fact that there, in that one person, Jesus Christ of Nazareth is God, the eternal Son, and yet there at the same time is the man Jesus, the carpenter. You cannot *understand* a thing like that, and yet there is the statement of Scripture. The eternal Son came out of the bosom of the Father and was incarnate as Jesus of Nazareth. The eternal Son came in the likeness of sinful flesh and dwelt in a human frame, and in some such way as that God dwells in us and we in Him.

We will have to go on dealing with this—I am simply giving an outline here—but that is the astounding and amazing thing that the Apostle tells us. Here is the practical import of it all: Do not seek for visions; do not covet audible voices; do not enter into anything where you anticipate something eerie. 'Beloved people,' said John; 'you have something infinitely greater than that. God, who is love, dwells in you! If you love the brethren, here is a certainty, here is an assurance.'

Let me put it like this: If I love the brethren, I have an assurance of God in this way: the very fact that I do love the brethren and that I am capable of loving them is in itself proof to me that God is and that God is love, because apart from the love of God in me I could not love the brethren. Man by nature does not love. You remember how John elaborates on that in the previous chapter,[3] where he has told us that 'this is the message that ye heard from the beginning, that we should love one another. Not as Cain, who was of that wicked one, and slew his brother.' That is the world; if the world hates you, that is the kind of thing the world does, and that is how we all are by nature.

If I find myself loving a person who is not lovable, if I find myself ever praying for someone who has been persecuting me and has been dealing with me despitefully, if I find myself helping someone who has done his or her best to harm me, if I find myself doing that, I know that God is love and that He is within me, because if He were not in me I would never do it. I do not want to do this by nature; so if I love the brethren, I have a certainty that God is love. 'No man hath seen God.' How may I know that God is and that God loves me and that God is love? Here is the answer: If we love one another, God dwells in us. I do not have visions, I do not hear audible voices, I do not seek some material substantiation of what I claim; but I have it within me. So God must be in me; otherwise I could never do what I am doing.

But, indeed, John goes one step further. He says, 'God dwelleth in us, and his love is perfected in us.' What a glorious statement that is, and it means this: The ultimate objective of God in sending His Son into this world to be the propitiation for our sins and to do all that He did—the ultimate objective was that God might make of us such people that we should love the brethren and love one another even as He has loved us.

Now that is glorious! God sent His Son into the world to die on the cross of Calvary not simply that He might make a way whereby you and I could be forgiven—thank God that is there, and it is the first thing, for without that we are altogether lost; but that was not the end. The end was this: God was anxious to perfect His love, and He perfects His love in us not so much by what it does externally as by what it does within us. In other words, show me a Christian man or woman who is loving the brethren in spite of everything that is so true of them, and *there* is a demonstration of the love of God in a human soul. God has so dealt with them that He has made of them people like Himself.

All this was put so perfectly by our Lord Himself in the Sermon on the Mount: 'Love your enemies, bless them that curse you, do good to them that hate you, and pray for them which despitefully use you, and persecute you.' 'What credit, what merit have you if you love those who love you? The heathen do that. You know the sort of love I am talking about,' said our Lord in effect. 'Be ye therefore perfect, even as your Father which is in heaven is perfect.' That is the way you are to love. You are to love as God loves. He sends the rain upon the just and the unjust and causes His sun to shine upon the evil and the good (Matt 5:43-48). That is what we are to do. God's love is perfected in us, and therefore we must be perfect, even as our Father in heaven is perfect—and that context is solely about loving one another. So, as we love the brethren we are manifesting and demonstrating God's ultimate objective in all that He did in the Lord Jesus Christ. He is producing a race, a humanity like Himself, a people set apart, men and women who can rise to this height and to this level, men and women who love even as God loves.

There, it seems to me, is what the Apostle is telling us in this particular twelfth verse. We have started this new theme of assurance of salvation, this certainty of our fellowship and our relationship to God; and the first way to make sure of it and to know it is to love one another, to love the brethren. If I am loving the brethren, then I know that God must be in me, for otherwise I could not do it, and I am demonstrating God's ultimate eternal objective in sending His only begotten Son into the world to make Him the propitiation for my sins.

What a glorious doctrine! Let us cease to ask for visible tangible signs; let us cease from maligning this glorious truth; and let us accept this simple yet profound teaching which tells us to our amazement that God dwells in us.

7

The Gift of God's Spirit

Hereby know we that we dwell in him, and he in us, because he hath given us of his Spirit.

1 JOHN 4:13

In this verse John continues the theme which has really been occupying him from the beginning of verse 7–the importance of loving one another. The reason, he says, for stressing this is that it is only as we love one another that we truly come to know God, and that is the most important thing of all. And the great basis of a true knowledge of God in this world and life is to know in that way that God is dwelling in us and we in God. John, therefore, is now suggesting to us various tests by which we may know this. And John in the twelfth verse gives us the first test: Are we loving one another? If we find that we are loving our Christian brothers and sisters, then we can be certain that God is in us, because apart from God dwelling in us there is no love in us.

Then here, in this thirteenth verse, John comes to the second great proof which we have of the fact that God is dwelling in us and we in God, and here it is: 'Hereby know we that we dwell in him, and he in us, because he hath given us of his Spirit.'

Now it is very interesting to observe the way in which John probably arrived at this statement. I think he must have done so like this: He has been talking about this love which we should have for one another, and then he asks himself, 'But where does this love come from?' And he is at once reminded that it comes from the Holy Spirit. As Paul says, 'The love of God is shed abroad in our hearts by the Holy Ghost which is given to us' (Rom 5:5). John has been talking about this love; well, the possession of this love means the possession of the Spirit. And that is the second test.

It seems to me that there are three main things stated in this verse. Firstly, we are reminded of the nature of the Christian life. I start with this because I am increasingly convinced that most of our troubles arise from the fact that our whole conception of the Christian life tends to be inadequate. I am not referring to people outside the church at the moment, but to Christian people. I speak for myself when I say that there is nothing of which I have to remind myself more constantly than the very nature of the Christian life. We are all the same; the first Christians were the same as well, and that is why the epistles were written. It was because of this constant tendency to think and conceive of the Christian life in an inadequate manner that the Apostles were led and moved by God to write their letters with their wonderful instruction.

We always tend to narrow down the Christian life. There are so many people who still seem to think of it as if it were a question of giving up two or three particularly gross and obvious sins and attending a place of worship; but how unworthy and inadequate a view that is! So let us start by means of a negative. What is the Christian life? What does it mean to be a Christian? What is the essential nature of this life to which we are called? Let me remind you again of certain things which are hopelessly inadequate. Living as a Christian does not just mean moral living, nor just being good and decent. Of course it includes those things, but that is not the whole of the Christian life.

I start with that because is it not obvious that there are large numbers of people who think seriously that that constitutes the Christian life? There are many people attending morning services in church who say that just because they are not guilty of certain things, they are true Christians. To which I reply, 'Hereby know we that we dwell in him, and he in us, because he hath given us of his Spirit'; then their little morality shrivels into nothing. Morality is essential, but God forbid that we should reduce this glorious thing and this glorious life to just a little decency and morality!

Or there are those who think of it in terms of high ideals. There is a great deal of this being noised abroad at the present time. There are various movements which I regard as nothing but an equating of the Christian life with the holding of certain high ideals. And people think that by preaching them, every workman will be prepared to work twenty-four hours a day because he is animated by these noble ideals, all in the name of Christianity. As if that were the total of Christianity! There are thoughts associated with Christianity, the highest and noblest thoughts that have ever come to man; but if we equate them with what we are told here, then we are merely in possession of certain high ideals and are insulting the work of our blessed Lord and Saviour Jesus Christ.

Then there are those who think of Christianity just as a matter of religious conformity. They actually believe that they are Christians and others are not simply because they conform to certain habits and practices. They attend a morning service, and then they may do anything they like for the rest of the day; that morning service has made them Christian. They are conforming to a certain conduct and behaviour, and that, to them, is the Christian life. And because other people do not do all this, they look at them and say, 'We are different; we are doing something they are not'—religious conformity. Of course, again it is obvious that this is part of the Christian life, but to regard that as the whole of it is to miss the splendour and the glory and the wonder of this great thing that is expounded in the new Testament.

Or let me go one step further and say that a general belief in the Christian message does not make one a Christian. Obviously this again is essential, but merely to subscribe to certain tenets of the faith does not make us Christians; that is one of the preliminary conditions, but it is not the thing itself. To believe certain things about God and Christ in and of itself does not make one a Christian; there is something higher than that, and here it is: '*Hereby* know we that we dwell in him, and he in us'–that is the nature of the Christian life. We saw this in verse 12 where John says, 'If we love one another, God dwelleth in us.' We saw that this is something that eludes definition and understanding in a sense, and yet it is something very definite, and John amplifies it here. Not only does He dwell in us, but we dwell in Him. This is an amazing, mystical relationship with God into which we have been brought by the Lord Jesus Christ and His perfect work. What does this mean? It means that we are in a living relationship with God; that is why I have contrasted it with believing certain things *about* God. There is all the difference in the world between these two things.

Have we not known this experience? There is a stage in which we believe certain things about God and Christ, but we do not know Him. When we went on our knees to pray, we felt there was a distance, a strangeness, an uncertainty. How different that is from knowing that we are in a vital relationship with God, being aware of the fact that somehow we are participating in the life of God and that God is in our life. There is a change in us–we are not merely ourselves; there is this other factor. We know that this is not merely a question of intellectual acceptance; it is not a question of our just doing duties or merely in a mechanical way saying our prayers or something like that. No. We are aware of being in a living relationship to God; there is something vital about our whole position, and we are aware of the fact that in some astounding manner we are, in reality, sharing the life of God Himself. As Peter puts it, we are made 'partakers of'–we are sharing in–'the divine nature.'

Now we must be careful not to materialise this, and we must not reduce it. So I am anxious to emphasise again that when we consider these other conceptions of the Christian life—that morality, those high ideals, that noble conception of life and the high sense of duty and religious conformity and even an intellectual belief—we should see how inadequate are all those put together when we come to this. Here we are taken up into the life of God! Because, you see, in those discourses of His just before the end, our Lord talked about the Father and Himself abiding in us—God dwelling in us; 'Abide in me and I in you.' That is the Christian life; nothing less than that must ever satisfy us, and we must never conceive of it in any terms that are lower than that.

That brings me to my second proposition, which is that we may know, and should know, that we are in that relationship to God and that we possess that life. That is the nature of the Christian life. 'Hereby,' says John, '*know we*'—we know it, and we are certain of it. I have often, in dealing with this epistle, pointed out that this is, for John, one of the greatest things of all. He has told us several times, and he will tell us again before we have finished, that his whole business in writing this letter is that we may have this knowledge: 'These things have I written unto you that believe on the name of the Son of God; that ye may know that ye have eternal life, and that ye may believe on the name of the Son of God' (5:13).

Now we all possess this knowledge, and we must never be satisfied with anything less than that. I put it like that because I know a number of friends who really are opposed to such teaching. I remember once saying something along this line in a different connection and afterwards having a conversation with a good man who had been present at the service.

He said, 'Don't you think you were a little bit hard on us this afternoon?'

'Why?' I asked.

'Well,' he said, 'you said that *all* of us ought to have this knowledge of God.'

'Certainly,' I replied. 'Wasn't I explaining my text?'

'Ah, yes,' he said. 'I believe Peter and John and Paul should have had this knowledge, but surely not all of us ordinary Christians.'

And then he proceeded really to defend his own ignorance and regarded my saying that every Christian should have this knowledge as a hard statement.

But this knowledge is to me the very essence of the New Testament teaching. What the Bible offers us is nothing less than this knowledge that God is in us and we in Him, and we should not rest for a moment until we have it. We have no right to be uncertain—'that ye may *know*.' Christians who are uncertain of where they are, are doing dishonour to the gospel of Jesus Christ, to the work of Christ upon the cross, and to His glorious resurrection. We must not rest until we have full and certain assurance, confidence, and jubilation. The whole of the New Testament has been written in order that we may have it, and I argue that this is something that really must be inevitable. I cannot understand anyone who not only lacks this certainty, but who would even be prepared to argue against such a certainty. I cannot understand such a person, even on the grounds of logic.

Let me put it in this way: As unbelievers we were dead; we had no spiritual life. A Christian must be born again, by faith, in order to have the life of God in his soul. So, is it possible that we can have such life in us and not know it? I say that is impossible! The presence of the life of God in our soul is so different from the life without God that we cannot but know it; and therefore if you are uncertain, you must examine the foundation of your life. For this is what is offered: nothing less than that God will come to dwell in us and will take us into Himself; so we must know this, we may know it, and we can thank God we can know it.

This brings me to my last proposition, which is the way in which we may have this knowledge. 'Hereby know we that we dwell in him, and he in us.' How? The answer is, '*because he hath given us of his Spirit*.' So it all comes down to that in the last analysis. How do I know that I have received God's Spirit? How may I know for certain that I have been given and receive something of the Holy Spirit of God? Now this is a great subject, and I can only touch on it briefly. Let me say as a word of warning that there is a great danger of confining this whole teaching concerning the Holy Spirit to particular aspects only or to particular results of the gift of the Holy Spirit. Let me just suggest to you certain tests which we all should apply to ourselves in order that we may know that we have received the Holy Spirit—this gift of God.

Here are some of them. I shall start at the lowest and rise to the highest, and I do that for the good reason that if you can say 'Yes' to my first test, then you can be happy that you have received the Holy Spirit. So I start with this: Are you concerned about these things, and have you a desire to have them? Are these things of great concern to you—are they the things that interest you? I often notice when traveling by train that there are large numbers of people who seem to be first of all interested, and tremendously interested, in the latest murder or something like that. They rush for the paper, and they want to read all the latest news. Is that the limit of your interest, or are you interested in other things? Are you concerned about the life of your soul? Are you concerned about knowing God? Are you interested in eternity? Are these the things that interest you? I assure you that if they are, the Holy Spirit is in you, for people apart from God 'mind earthly things' (Phil 3:19)—carnal, fleshly things. It may not always be murder; it may be the Royal Family; it may be in what is happening in so-called high society and all the pomp and show of life. It is the same thing—it is the same interest in the last analysis. Is that the limit of your interest, or is your interest spiritual? Are you concerned about immortality and the things invisible and eternal? If you are 'minding' these things, that is a proof that the Holy Spirit is in you.

Or let me hurry on to another test: a sense of sin. By this I mean that you are aware that there is an evil principle within you—not simply that you do certain things you should not do and feel annoyed with yourself because of it. No; rather, I mean that you are aware that you have an evil nature, that there is a principle of sin and wrong in your heart, that there is a fountain emitting unworthy, ugly, and foul things, and in a sense you hate yourself. Our Lord said that the man who loves himself is in a very dangerous condition. The Apostle Paul was a man who could say about himself, 'In me (that is, in my flesh,) dwelleth no good thing. . . . O wretched man that I am!' (Rom 7:18, 24). Have you ever felt like that about yourself? If you have, you can take it from me that the Holy Spirit is in you; no man or woman has said this until God the Holy Spirit has come into them. So if you have ever felt yourself a sinner, and if you have hated this thing in you that gets you down, that is a proof that you have received the gift of the Holy Spirit.

What else? A belief on the Lord Jesus Christ. I need not stay with that here because we will come to it in verses 14-15. But I just mention it now as something essential. Paul says in writing to the Corinthians that the princes of this world did not recognise Him when He came (1 Cor 2:8). Why? Because they did not have the Holy Spirit. But we do believe, because we have received the Spirit, and 'the Spirit searcheth all things, yea, the deep things of God' (1 Cor 2:10). Anyone who believes truly on the Lord Jesus Christ has received the gift of the Spirit.

But I must hurry on to another test. Are you aware within yourself of a struggle and a conflict between the flesh and the Spirit? Paul deals with that in Galatians 5: 'The flesh lusteth against the Spirit, and the Spirit against the flesh' (v 17). He means this: Are you aware of two opposing natures within you? It is not merely that occasionally you want to do things that are wrong and have to struggle in your mind; no, it is deeper than that. Are you aware of the fact that really in a sense you are two people? There is a new kind of person in you who wants these heavenly, spiritual things; but there is another who wants to get you down, and there is a struggle and conflict one against the other. According to the Scriptures, that is one of the best tests of whether the Holy Spirit is in you. If you are in a state of conflict with these opposing forces, you can be quite sure the Holy Spirit is in you, because without the Holy Spirit there is no such conflict—it is all the 'old man.' But if you are having a conflict between the new and the old, then you know the Holy Spirit is indeed within you.

Let me take it a step further. Are you aware of the fact that God is working in you? 'Work out your own salvation with fear and trembling,' says Paul, 'for it is God which worketh in you both to will and to do' (Phil 2:12-13). This is a marvelous, wonderful thing. It is one of the great tests of the possession of the Holy Spirit. It means something like this: We are aware of the fact that we are being dealt with; it is not that we decide to do things. You see, moralists and religious conformists are doing it all themselves, and that is why they are so proud of themselves. They get up on Sunday mornings instead of spending the morning in bed, and they go to church. They do it because *they* have decided to do it, not because they have been moved. No, they are in control the whole time; and having done it, they preen themselves with their wonderful, ennobling ideals. How marvelous they are!

But that is not what the Bible talks about. 'It is God which worketh in you both to will and to do.' In other words, you are aware of the power of God dealing with you, surging and rising within you, and you are amazed and astonished at yourself. Far from being proud you say, 'It is not I. This is not the sort of person I am. It is God doing something; it is Christ dwelling within me; it is the Holy Spirit that is in me. I am taken up beyond myself, and I thank God for it.' Is God working in you? Are you aware of a disturbance in your life? Are you aware of a wonder-working power active in you, moving, disturbing, leading, persuading, drawing you ever onwards? If you are, it is because you have received from God the gift of His own Spirit. God is resident within you, and He is working out His own grand purpose in you in that way.

And that brings me to the next great test, which is again to be found in Galatians 5—that which Paul describes as 'the fruit of the Spirit.' The Spirit is life, and life always manifests itself in some shape or form as fruit; a live tree bears fruit, a dead tree does not. These are scriptural analogies, and I have nothing to do at this point but to remind you of what Paul tells us about the fruit of the Spirit. 'The fruit of the Spirit is love, joy, peace, long-suffering, gentleness, goodness, faith, meekness, temperance' (Gal 5:22-23). The way to test whether the Holy Spirit is in you is to examine yourself, your own life, and to discover whether there is any evidence or manifestation of such fruit.

Do you know that the Holy Spirit cannot be in you without that fruit appearing? I know there is a great variation in the fruit. In the Parable of the Sower we read that there is some thirty, some sixty, some a hundredfold; but thank God, even the thirty proves that the Holy Spirit is there. Even ten would prove it; even one. Thank God for that! Not that I am to rest with the tenfold, but thank God for the assurance that any fruit at all proves that He is there. 'Love, joy, peace, long-suffering, gentleness, goodness, faith, meekness, temperance'—are these things in us? Are they being evidenced in our lives? If they are, the Holy Spirit is in us, and we are becoming more and more like the Lord Jesus Christ. In a sense, that is the most perfect description of Him that you will find anywhere—that ninefold fruit, the three groups of three. This is the description of Jesus Christ. Love—there it was to be seen in His life; the love of God incarnate. Joy—that holy joy in spite of everything. That peace that never forsook Him. Gentleness, goodness, meekness . . . And as the Holy Spirit is resident in us and produces this fruit, we become more and more like Christ. This is the fruit of the Spirit.

Then the next thing I would mention is the Spirit of adoption. You remember how Paul works that out in Romans 8. Because we have received the Spirit, we 'have received the Spirit of adoption, whereby we cry, Abba, Father' (v 15). God is no longer some distant potentate in eternity. He has become a Father to us; and when we come to Him, we feel we come to our Father, the Father of the prodigal, and we come without fear. John elaborates that toward the end of this chapter when he says that there is 'no fear in love'; we will come to that. But to know God and to see 'Abba, Father' in the Lord Jesus Christ and to know ourselves to be His child—do you know Him like that?

And lastly I would mention the various gifts of the Spirit, the various powers the Spirit may give us. You can read the list in 1 Corinthians 12. You may have some of them—you may have one of them, or you may have more. That chapter does not say that every Christian has them all. Paul goes out of his way to say that. Not all have the gift of prophecy; all cannot speak and preach; there is variation; and they are dispensed according to His sovereignty. He may give us the gifts, or He may not. 'And yet,' says Paul, 'show I unto you a more excellent way' (1 Cor 12:31). The gifts of the Spirit—what are they? They are all summed up in one word: *love*. The fruit of the Spirit is love pre-eminently; and if we have that, then we have that final and ultimate proof: 'Hereby know we that we dwell in him, and he in us, because he hath given us of his Spirit.' Do you know this? Have you received this gift of God's Spirit? I have reminded you of the tests; if you have them, God bless you. Now go on to covet the best gifts more and more; long increasingly for the fruit of the Spirit; and ask God to work more and more in you.

If, having listened to all this, you have come to the conclusion that you have not received the gift of God's Spirit, then all I say to you is what our Lord Jesus Christ said: 'If ye then, being evil, know how to give good gifts unto your children; how much more shall your heavenly Father give the Holy Spirit to them that ask him?' (Luke 11:13). If you feel you have not got this gift, and if you long to possess this priceless possession, go to God without delay. Acknowledge your bankruptcy, confess your emptiness, ask Him to have mercy upon you, plead His own promise, and go on asking until you receive it. For the promises of God are ever sure, and we have His gracious, blessed word: 'Him that cometh to me I will in no wise cast out' (John 6:37). Ask Him, and if you ask and seek and knock, you shall receive a great and glorious abundance.

'Blessed are they which do hunger and thirst after righteousness: for they shall be filled' (Matt 5:6); they shall be filled with the fullness of God Himself.

8
The Fullness of Blessing

Hereby know we that we dwell in him, and he in us, because he hath given us of his Spirit.

1 JOHN 4:13

This was written by an Apostle of Jesus Christ to men and women in a very troubled and perplexing world, towards the end of the first century. The world then was a difficult place, just as it is today—full of troubles and contradictions, full of confusion. It has always been like that. There have been periods of comparative peace, but the world has always been a hard, trying place, and in a sense we can never truly understand the message of the Bible unless we realise that the various books of the Bible were written in a world like that. Our danger in every generation is to think of our immediate perplexities as being quite exceptional; yet any reading of biography or of history should clear our minds of any such idea, for we find that men and women have always regarded their particular era as an unusual and particularly difficult one. Thus we must always bear that in mind as a kind of background to our consideration.

So here, as we have seen, is an old man writing just before he leaves this world, and he gives his final words of advice to men and women who will go on living after his departure. He is concerned about them, he is vitally interested, he wants to help them, and yet what does he write to them? Well, he does not attempt any evaluation of the political situation, nor does he deliver a number of pompous generalities and vague and pious hopes and aspirations. There is, in a sense, no reference to the political or international situation. Rather, he writes to them individually and directly. He does say something about the world, but what he says about it is, 'We know that we are of God, and the whole world lieth in wickedness' (5:19). So according to this man the question is, what are we doing in such a world? What can be done for us? What is most important for us?

Now, it seems to me that we are in precisely that situation. We are all aware of the world in which we live and its condition and its trouble, but the question is, what has the Christian Church to say in the midst of all this? What is the message to Christian people at this point? And if we want to be true to the New Testament we must do exactly what it does. We all have our opinions, and I suppose we are ready to argue for our opinion, and yet surely this century should have taught us that we waste a good deal of time in our prophecies and forebodings concerning the future. We know so little, and our prognostications are almost invariably wrong. Surely, therefore, the great thing for us is rather to view all these things in the light of the teaching of the Scriptures themselves; and as I understand the teaching of the Bible it comes to this, that whatever people may say and whatever may be held out as hopes before us, this world is a place of sin.

This has been so throughout the centuries—look at the long history that is recorded in the Bible. The world has been a place of woe and a place of warfare, misery, unhappiness, and wretchedness, and in spite of all that we were told in the last century as to how different the world was going to be in the twentieth century, we have lived to see that the world is still the same. Therefore, it seems to me to be utterly unchristian and completely contradictory to the message of Scripture to attempt to put forward solutions which are somehow or another going to put this world right, because the whole message of the Bible is to show that this cannot happen. The essence of wisdom, according to Scripture, is that we should make certain that we are not involved in the perdition of this world which is coming, but that rather we should be saved out of it and should be reconciled to God.

That is the message of this Book from beginning to end. The people in whom the Bible glories are men and women who set their gaze upon another world. That was the great secret of Abraham. He did not become immersed and involved in the political situation of the cities of the plain; he was a man who 'looked for a city which hath foundations, whose builder and maker is God' (Heb 11:10). Such people, we are told, are strangers on the earth; they are men and women who are set apart in life and who have learned that the vital thing is their relationship to God. They make sure that in spite of the world that is around and about them they are not involved finally in the catastrophe that is to overwhelm it because of sin.

And thus it seems to me that the whole principle of Christian preaching is not to express vague, general, contradictory ideas as to what should happen. Let us, rather, come to something of which we are certain, and what we are certain of is that the whole world is to be judged by God, that no one can escape Him, and that there is but one way to be reconciled to God, and that is in and through our Lord Jesus Christ. We know that we need to be delivered out of this world; we know the whole world is passing away. It is not for me to try to predict what the next year will hold for all of us—we do not know; but what I do know is that if I am right with God in Christ, I can face whatever happens, and I can say with the great Apostle that 'I am persuaded, that neither death, nor life, nor angels, nor principalities, nor powers, nor things present, nor things to come, nor height, nor depth, nor any other creature, shall be able to separate us from the love of God, which is in Christ Jesus our Lord' (Rom 8:38-39).

Can *we* say that? Are *we* in that position? That is the question! That is the theme, as we have seen, of this particular section of 1 John 4. The knowledge of God—that is the thing, says John, that we may know that we dwell in Him and He in us. How do we arrive at that knowledge?

I have pointed out that there are certain tests that we can apply to ourselves in order that we may know whether we have received the Spirit of God, the Holy Spirit. That is the most important question for anyone in this world today. It is infinitely more important than the question of whether there will be another war or not. Infinitely more important than the atomic bomb and its possible use is this question, have I received the Holy Spirit of God? For whether there is to be a war or not, I have got to meet God, and therefore the urgent question for me is, have I received His Spirit? Am I dwelling in God, and is God dwelling in me?

Now there are certain general tests that one can apply to oneself, and we have seen some already. A sense of sin, a sense of unworthiness, a realisation of who Jesus Christ is and what He has done, and an increasing longing to be more like Him—an awareness of a conflict between the flesh and the Spirit, this internal warfare—the fruit of the Spirit, and the possession, perhaps, of certain of the special gifts which the Holy Spirit in His sovereignty dispenses to certain people at certain times—these are the general tests. They are of vital importance, and we tried to look at them in their ascending order.

But I come back to this subject because it is such a vital one, and I return to it also because it does seem to be the subject which leads a great many people into confusion. It is a question which is frequently discussed among Christian people, this whole question of whether I have received the Holy Spirit. How can one receive the Holy Spirit, what does one do to receive the Spirit, and what are the manifestations of the Spirit in one's life and experience?

First of all, let us remind ourselves of what is possible for us as Christian people. Now, there is no question as to this when you read the pages of the New Testament itself. The picture there of the Christian is something that is perfectly clear and definite. The New Testament Christian is always someone who seems to know what he has; there is a clear division between the Christian and the non-Christian. The New Testament talks about those who belong to the world. It also talks about those who are in Christ, and you notice the assumptions which are constantly made by the writers of the various New Testament epistles. For example: 'Whom having not seen, ye love; in whom, though now ye see him not, yet believing, ye rejoice with joy unspeakable and full of glory' (1 Pet 1:8). That is the assumption that is made about Christians in the New Testament; they are people who glory in Christ—they love Him. The people described in this Book are people whom you can describe, if you like, as being 'pneumatic'; they are spiritual people. There is a new order, a new quality in their lives; they are not just ordinary people striving to be good. A life has been given to them; something has happened to them. They have received this gift of the Spirit of God; they are a changed and a different people.

Look at the first possessors of the Holy Spirit on the day of Pentecost. The people said, 'These men are drunk'; they were like men possessed. You cannot read the New Testament without gaining that impression. There was a power about them, a radiance, a newness, a love, a warmth and enthusiasm about them which was quite unmistakable, and that is why I say that as these letters were written to them, these great assumptions were so constantly made. The Christian is one set apart: a 'new man,' a 'new creation,' a 'new life.' Christians are people who give the impression that they have received something from above, and therefore they are so different.

Now this is something which is confirmed by the subsequent history of the church. You read about that history during any period of revival and reawakening and you will find exactly the same thing. There is this same quality of life and exuberance, this joy, this sense of exhilaration; in other words, the fruit of the Spirit, in all its aspects, is being manifested in the lives of Christian people at such times. In other words, when the Spirit of God comes into people's lives, that will of necessity make a difference; and thus we find it in the New Testament and in the history of the church at every period of revival and true life. The thing I am anxious to emphasise here is that the New Testament makes it very clear that that order and quality of life is possible for *all* Christians; it is not only for some. I defy anyone to give any statement in the New Testament which says that this particular order and quality of life is only meant for certain people.

Now there are many who hold that idea. They say, 'Yes, that is all right for certain exceptional people whom you may categorise as religious geniuses.' But the New Testament never says that. It is all-inclusive in its description. The Apostle Paul, for example, never said that he had something which no one else possessed. Indeed, he went out of his way to say the opposite in writing to the Roman Christians. He was anxious to visit them so that he could 'impart . . . some spiritual gift . . . that is, that I may be comforted together with you by the mutual faith both of you and me' (Rom 1:11-12). This is for all who are sinners saved by grace, all who respond to the same Holy Spirit.

In other words, the great message of the New Testament is that natural divisions and distinctions become comparatively unimportant. Because we all can possess and be filled by the Spirit of God, we share the same life and the same experience. Therefore, we must start with the proposition that this is something that is possible for all of us. So this comes back to us again as a very urgent question: Have I received the Holy Spirit? 'Hereby know we that we dwell in him, and he in us, because he hath given us of his Spirit.' Has God given me His Spirit? That is the question. Do I know that I am in God and God in me because I have received God's gift of His own Spirit?

Now, I say there are difficulties which confront certain people

THE FULLNESS OF BLESSING

as they face that question. There are many who are perplexed about this whole subject, and I suggest to you that there are three main causes of difficulty.

The first cause of difficulty I would describe as wrong teaching, and there are various kinds of false teaching with respect to this matter. There is, for instance, the idea that this receiving of the Holy Spirit is something that always happens suddenly. There are those who think that the Holy Ghost can only be received suddenly; further, because they never receive any sudden experience, they say that they have never received the Holy Spirit. Now there are instances in the Bible where people did receive the Holy Spirit suddenly, but there are also instances where people did not, and in the history of the church you find exactly the same thing. Attention always tends to be focused upon that which is most dramatic, and thus as you read books on this subject, you will find that they generally give a list of the people who received the sudden gift. But it is equally clear in the Bible and in the history of the church that the gift does not always come to individuals in a sudden and dramatic manner.

Or let me put it like this: There is a teaching which would have us believe that the Holy Spirit is always received with great emotional upheaval. Once more I think the reason is exactly the same. In some instances there was a remarkable, dramatic, and emotional experience; but it does not always happen in that way. I was reading recently what I regard as a most sane illustration of that point. It was an essay about that great man of God who was used so much in China, Jonathan Goforth. He tells us about his own experience. He thought that this gift of the Holy Spirit would come upon him as it did to men like Finney and D. L. Moody, who received the gift suddenly and with great emotional upheaval. Goforth thought that he would receive it in the same way. And yet he tells us that when he received this fullness of the Spirit there was no dramatic intensity, and he thanks God for that because, he says, 'If I had received this gift in the same way as Finney and Moody, then I would have been another wonder added to the list of those who had got it like that. But let me place on record that I have received the same gift and it came quite quietly to me and almost unconsciously. I became aware of the fact that God's Holy Spirit was resident in me and was filling me with power.' He was then led to take part in a great revival movement in China and various other parts of the Far East. That, I think, is a very salutary reminder of this great fact—it is not always a great emotional upheaval. What is important is not *how* but *whether* I receive it.

Then there are others who say we have nothing to do in the matter, and we receive the gift of the Holy Ghost passively. They say you must cease from striving; you become utterly passive, and in that passive condition you receive the gift of the Holy Ghost.

And lastly, I would say that the other wrong teaching is a failure to differentiate between the gift and the grace of the Holy Spirit. Once more it is very natural that we should look at that which is most dramatic, and some of the gifts of the Spirit are very dramatic: for example, the gifts of healing, the gifts of tongues, and the gifts of interpretation. We tend to concentrate upon these, but we must be clear in our minds that the Holy Spirit can come to us not only in outstanding gifts, but still more in what are called the graces of the Spirit. Paul gave us a list of the graces in 1 Corinthians 13. Let us realise that the Holy Spirit produces this wonderful fruit, the grace of the Lord Jesus Christ Himself, in the life of men and women.

Those, then, are some aspects of false teaching. But secondly, I suggest that there are others who are in difficulty about this matter because of wrong desires or wrong motives. Take, for example, the case that is cited in Acts 8, that of the man called Simon. He had listened to the preaching of Philip and of Peter and John, and he had seen how Peter and John prayed that the gift of the Holy Ghost might descend upon the believers. And when Simon saw that through the laying of the Apostles' hands upon them they received the Holy Spirit, he coveted that power for himself, and he wanted to buy the power and so be able to give that wonderful blessing to others. His motive was wrong; his desire was wrong. And many of us have to plead guilty of that very thing. So often we desire particular feelings or particular experiences; so often we desire particular gifts.

That is one of the dangers in reading Christian literature, as I have already been indicating. We read about Finney or about Moody, and we say, 'Wouldn't it be wonderful to have an experience like that!' But we must not covet experiences; we must not covet gifts. Rather, we are to covet and desire righteousness; we are to covet holiness. What we should desire is not that we may have some great flashing experience, or that we may have some great miracle-working gift, or the gift of speech, or any other gift; we should desire earnestly that gift that would most make us like the Lord Jesus Christ. We should desire to be the kind of person that is described in Romans 12. That is what we should covet; we must hunger and thirst after righteousness, not after blessing. And if we do so, we shall obtain the blessing, we shall be blessed, we shall be filled, we shall receive this gift of the Holy Spirit. Therefore, we must be careful to examine our motives and desires, and we must be perfectly certain that we do not just desire to be like somebody else who was known to be a remarkable Christian, so that our names will go down in church history, and people will point to us and say what remarkable and wonderful persons we were. All that, of course, would quench the Spirit; the motive is wrong, and the desire is false.

My third heading would be wrong practice, and wrong practice is summarised in the New Testament in this way: We are perhaps not aware of the Holy Spirit within us because we are guilty of quenching the Spirit. That may mean not obeying the prompting of the Holy Spirit within us. The Holy Spirit may have come into our lives quite quietly and unobtrusively, and He is resident within us and moving us and prompting us; not to obey His prompting, not to yield to it, is to quench the Holy Spirit. And if we are quenching the Spirit, we will not be aware of the power and the life and activity of the Spirit in our lives.

Perhaps one of the ways of doing this today is by what I would call intellectualism, and this is something about which some of us have to be very careful. There are those perhaps who have enough discrimination to see that what so often is claimed to be a gift of the Holy Spirit is nothing but a riot of the emotions. There are those who having read and studied can say of certain people who claim to be filled with the Holy Spirit that their fleshly character is obvious. It is quite clear that they are suffering from some emotional complex. But the danger to such critics is that they could be so afraid of having something like that that they actually quench the Holy Spirit within them. They can be so afraid of the false that they even miss the true, and therefore I would say to all who are intellectual and who are concerned about these things that we must beware of quenching the Spirit and of reducing the gospel of Jesus Christ to a mere intellectual proposition. This is *life*; it moves, it disturbs, it fills with love and joy and makes people enthusiastic. Those New Testament Christians, and the history of revivals, prove that. Let us be careful that in our fear of emotionalism we do not fall into the same error as the church of the eighteenth century which condemned Whitefield and others as mere enthusiasts and failed to recognise them as men who had been filled with the Spirit of God. This is quenching the Spirit!

The other way in which we engage in wrong practise is to grieve the Spirit. 'Grieve not the Holy Spirit,' says the Scripture (Eph 4:30). We grieve the Spirit by committing sin, by being disobedient to God's holy law. So if you want to know that the Spirit of God is in you, you must not sin. Sin grieves the Spirit; to do deliberately that which you know to be wrong is to be in the position in which you cannot know that the Holy Spirit is in you. So if there is anything doubtful in your life, you must get rid of it, for while there is any doubt, the Holy Spirit will not manifest Himself.

These, then, are some of the causes of difficulty, but let me hurry to a positive point. If those are the causes of difficulty, how does one obtain a fullness of the Spirit? How can we be sure that the Holy Spirit dwells in us? Well, you do not remain passive—you do certain things. First of all, you read the Bible. I put that first because I regard it of first importance. It is only as we fill ourselves with the Word of God that we shall really know what is possible to us; it is as I read this New Testament day by day that I see more and more the possibilities for every Christian. It is only as I read this Word that I shall be guarded against error. It is those who do not read it who are misled by the false. If we keep to the Word, there are tests that can be applied, there are proofs that can be given. The reading of the Bible must come first. Go again through the lives of the people throughout the centuries, and you will find that they always did that. They read the Word of God, and they saw what was possible to them as they read it, and they said, 'Oh, that I had that gift!' Read it, and you will see the difference between the true and the false.

Then secondly, I would mention obedience; we must avoid grieving the Spirit, and we must avoid quenching the Spirit. We must humble ourselves, as the Scriptures exhort us to. Scripture has told us that we must not think more highly of ourselves than we ought to think (Rom 12:3); this is a danger confronting us all. The Bible tells us to humble ourselves and not to overestimate ourselves. It tells us to 'mortify' the flesh, to wage a warfare, to battle against everything that tends to drag us down. 'Mortify therefore your members which are upon the earth,' says Scripture (Col 3:5), and we ought to do that actively. We are also to obey every prompting and leading of the Spirit and every holy desire and aspiration and every urge to prayer; all these things must be immediately obeyed—that is the instruction of Scripture.

And then next I cite that which in a sense makes these first two really possible—namely, prayer, an earnest desire for this, petitioning and pleading before God for it. And we must go on with this; we must continue, and we must persist. Nothing comes out more clearly in Christian biographies than that. Take note of these men and women who received the gift; they tell you that they became dissatisfied; they saw that they were lacking in the centre of their being. They not only read the Scriptures, but they began to pray, and they prayed day by day. They pleaded with God; they asked for this fuller blessing of the Holy Spirit, and they went on and on and on until they received the answer that they desired—prayer, pleading, continuously imploring God to grant them this great blessing.

And I close with another practical word: How does this blessing come? Well, I do not see any evidence in the New Testament to support what used to be called a 'tarrying meeting.' Some people had that idea. God had certain blessings to give, and they thought they had to wait until they received them. But the gift is given by God in His own way and time; this gift does not come of necessity at once. It is God's gift, and He knows when to give it and when to withhold it.

Here once more it seems to me that history is very helpful. Do you remember the case of Moody? This was his story. He became conscious of his lack and need, and he began to pray to God about it. He gave obedience to the Word of God as well as he could, and he went on praying for months. Nothing happened to him, but still he went on praying. Yes, he waited for it, but it did not come, and the story is that one day, walking down a street in New York, not in a tarrying meeting, not even in a prayer meeting, suddenly God overwhelmed him with this mighty blessing. It was so mighty that Moody felt he must be killed by it, and he held up his hand and said, 'Stop, God!'

God has His own time. Thank God that He knows us better than we know ourselves! Some of us have asked for great gifts and, thank God, He has not given them to us; we would have spent them upon our own lusts. I think that every Christian, looking back, must thank God that certain things were withheld in his or her life and experience. If God gave certain gifts to some of us, we would consume them in our own self-glorification; but thank God, He withholds them. Some of us perhaps need to be humbled; some of us need to be brought to the very dust. God knows when to give the gift, and we must never imagine that by going to a meeting or following a certain procedure it is bound to come. No; the Holy Spirit is sovereign, and He gives in His own way. It may be dramatically or suddenly or quietly; that is irrelevant, because what really matters is that we receive the gift.

The essence of it all, I think, can be put very simply: 'Trust and obey.' If we realise that there is this difference between us and those New Testament Christians, and if we long to be like them, we shall persist in reading this Word and in giving obedience to everything we discover in it; and we shall pray to God to shed His love abroad in our hearts and to give us His own gracious, glorious fullness. We shall go on and on, and as we do so God will answer us; of that we can be certain. This is God's will, even our sanctification. He is anxious to bless us and to give us this gift more than any human father is anxious for the well-being of his own child. God desires that we be filled with His own fullness; so let us ask Him, and let us leave the time and manner to Him and to Him alone. 'Blessed are they which do hunger and thirst after righteousness: for they shall be filled' (Matt 5:6). If I truly desire to be holy, if I desire to be like Christ and to do my utmost to be that and to look to God for the enabling for that, God will give me this fullness, this gift of the Holy Ghost, and I shall be filled. And then I shall know for certain that I dwell in Him and He in me because He has given me of His Spirit.

I say again, the most important thing in the world at this moment is to know we possess this gift. Has God given you His Holy Spirit? Oh, that we may come in simplicity to this Christian way and follow the simple steps that will certainly lead us to the fullness of blessing.

9

The Apostolic Witness and Testimony

And we have seen and do testify that the Father sent the Son to be the Saviour of the world. Whosoever shall confess that Jesus is the Son of God, God dwelleth in him, and he in God. And we have known and believed the love that God hath to us. God is love; and he that dwelleth in love dwelleth in God, and God in him.

1 JOHN 4:14–16

We come here to another of those great and magnificent statements which are such a characteristic feature of this first epistle of John. We have noticed as we have gone through the letter that ever and again these mighty statements of the gospel apparently suddenly appear and lift us to the heights. I constantly feel as I read and study this particular epistle that it is remarkably like a mountain range. You know how, when looking at a great range of mountains, you observe that while the total elevation is high, there are occasional peaks that stand out above the others and suddenly tower out in their magnificence. I feel that this letter is remarkably like that. The whole letter—every statement—is at that elevation, that great spiritual height, and ever and again as we look at it we suddenly observe these particular statements that seem to stand out with exceptional glory and wonder. We have already found several such in this very chapter.

Yet nothing is more important than that we should remember that this statement is in intimate association and connection with everything that is around it, and that is why a systematic study of Scripture is always ultimately the only true and fair and legitimate way of approaching it. We could take a verse like this and deal with it and preach on it in and of itself, and of course there would be a purpose in doing so; but if we want to understand its true significance, we must take it in its context, and that is why I feel the comparison of the great mountain range is very helpful. These verses must be taken together; verse 14 must be taken with verse 15, and 15 with 14, and verses 14 and 15 must be taken with the preceding verses and with the following verses, because they are all part of an argument in the Apostle's great statement.

John does not merely throw out statements like this at random; this is not something that suddenly juts out without any explanation or without any apparent rhyme or reason. He is working out an argument, as we have seen, and this is an essential part of his whole argument and position. The theme that engages us here is this whole theme of the assurance of salvation. He arrived at it by talking again about the importance of loving the brethren, and he says that if we do not love the brethren, that means we do not know God. That in turn leads him to talk about this subsidiary theme of knowing God; and that, according to John, is the most important thing in this world, that I should know that God is in me and I am in God.

Now here in verses 14 and 15 he goes to his next test as to how I can know this, and the main text as such is in verse 15: 'Whosoever shall confess that Jesus is the Son of God, God dwelleth in him, and he in God.' That is the third way in which I may know that I am in Him: loving the brethren, possessing the Holy Spirit, and confessing that Jesus is the Son of God. What he is concerned about is to show us and to explain to us how one can arrive in the position in which one can make this great confession.

So the test we must consider here is this one: Do I confess that Jesus is the Son of God? If I do, then I know that God is dwelling in me and I in God. That seems a simple statement, and yet I think we shall find it is a very profound one. I suggest, therefore, that we approach verses 14-15 in the light of these propositions.

First of all, I would state that a correct belief is proof of the possession of the Holy Spirit. John is really dealing here in essence with the doctrine of the Holy Spirit, and what the Holy Spirit in us enables us to do. His argument, in a sense, is that if we confess that Jesus is the Son of God, we do so because the Holy Spirit is enabling us to do so, and that means that the Holy Spirit must be in us; and as he has proved, if the Holy Spirit is in me, then I am in God and God is in me. That is the argument, but I think at this point that it is important that we should perhaps put it like this—namely, that a correct belief is impossible apart from the Holy Spirit.

I think John is anxious to put it as strongly as that, and here again we see how John by proceeding in this order corrects some of the false teachings that are current with regard to this whole doctrine of the Holy Spirit. There are people who do not hesitate to teach that you can be in a position in which you believe that Jesus is the Son of God and then later on you receive the Holy Spirit—that it is possible to be a believer without having received the Holy Spirit. Clearly by this particular passage that is an utter impossibility. John's whole case is that you cannot believe that Jesus is the Son of God unless God dwells in you and you in God; that is his argument. 'Whosoever shall confess that Jesus is the Son of God, God dwelleth in him, and he in God.' And the way in which God dwells in us is by the Holy Spirit. So we can say that the people who do confess that Jesus is the Son of God have the Holy Spirit already within them. Or to put it another way, they cannot believe that Jesus is the Son of God without possessing the Holy Spirit.

Now this is a doctrine which is common to the whole of the New Testament. The Apostle Paul puts it like this: 'We speak the wisdom of God in a mystery, even the hidden wisdom, which God ordained before the world unto our glory: which none of the princes of this world knew: for had they known it, they would not have crucified the Lord of glory. . . . But God hath revealed them unto us by his Spirit: for the Spirit searcheth all things, yea, the deep things of God' (1 Cor 2:7-8, 10).

You see, the whole case can be put like this: Even the princes of this world, the great men of the world, the mighty and the noble and the wise, looked at Jesus of Nazareth and saw nothing but a man, a carpenter, an artisan. They may have regarded Him as a kind of unusual religious genius, but they did not know He was the Lord of glory. Why not? Well, says Paul, because they had not received the Holy Spirit. But you and I, he says to the Corinthians, we understand these things, we believe them. Why? Because God has revealed them to us by His Spirit, the Spirit who searches all things, 'yea, the deep things of God.'

And then in 1 Corinthians 12:3 he again puts it in a very categorical statement. 'No man,' he says, 'can say that Jesus is the Lord, but by the Holy Ghost.' He cannot do it otherwise; it is impossible. So the way in which John puts it comes to this, that if a man does say that Jesus is the Lord, it must mean that the Holy Spirit is already resident within him. Thus I lay down this first proposition, that a correct belief, a true belief, is proof of the fact that we do, in entirety, possess the Holy Spirit; it is the Holy Spirit alone who can enable us to believe truly, and without the Holy Spirit we cannot believe.

Now this, of course, is something that can be seen very clearly in the history of the church, as it can in the Bible. It is seen in church history as a message preached to men and women, and there are those who believe it and those who do not. Here is a message which has been presented to men and women of intellect and understanding and great wisdom and knowledge, people who have been famous for their sanity and balance. They have heard it, and they have seen nothing in it. But on the other hand, you have some of the humblest and most ignorant and untutored and unlettered people who have heard it and rejoiced in it and who have been transformed by it and have become saints in the Church of God. To what is the difference due? What is the explanation? The explanation, says Scripture, is that the Holy Spirit has enabled these people to see and believe.

This teaching that you can believe first and then go on to receive the Spirit is utterly unscriptural. Of course, probably what such friends mean is that one can go on to have deeper and greater experiences of the Holy Spirit, but if that is what they mean, then let them say so; there is no such thing as belief apart from receiving the Holy Ghost. We can go on to receive a greater fullness. We can do that many times in our lives—we *should* be doing so; but what is fundamental is that the mere statement, in a true sense, that Jesus is the Son of God is proof positive that God dwells in us in His Holy Spirit and that we dwell in God.

There, surely, is something that ought to be of great comfort. There may be those who are very conscious of their imperfections, very conscious of their unworthiness, their faults and failures and sins. Now I am not anxious to administer false comfort, but I do say that whatever you may feel about yourself and however much you may be disposed to condemn yourself, if you really believe from your heart that Jesus is the Son of God, I assure you that God dwells in you and that God has given you His Holy Spirit, because you cannot believe it apart from that power which you have received.

Let us put that another way. A correct belief means an acceptance of the apostolic witness and testimony. That is what we mean by a correct belief. Now it is there that we see the importance of taking verses 14-15 together. 'And we . . .' says John, referring to himself and to his fellow Apostles and to those who are already Christians. He is referring to those of whom he speaks in the very introduction of the letter, where he says, 'That which we have seen and heard declare we unto you, that ye also may have fellowship with us: and truly our fellowship is with the Father, and with his Son Jesus Christ' (1:3). 'We,' says John here, 'have seen and do testify that the Father sent the Son to be the Saviour of the world.' Then he goes on to say, 'Whosoever therefore shall confess that Jesus is the Son of God, God dwelleth in him, and he in God.' So a correct belief comes to that; it is an acceptance of the apostolic witness and testimony.

This word 'confess' in verse 15 really means assenting unto, expressing my agreement, saying my 'Amen' to that which is said to me. I receive the statement, and I believe and accept it; that is what he means by confessing. Now here again surely is a vitally important statement. What makes men and women Christians is that they accept and subscribe to a certain body of teaching and doctrine concerning our Lord Jesus Christ. But how can they do that? What is it that enables them to make this confession that Jesus is the Son of God? On what ground do they make that statement?

Here it seems to me that there is only one answer given in the New Testament itself, and it is the one which I have already put to you. I can only confess in a true sense by accepting and believing the apostolic witness and testimony. I have not seen the Lord Jesus Christ with the eyes of flesh. I was not on the earth when He was here. So what do I know about Him? How can I believe in Him? Here we come back to this vital doctrine of the ultimate and final authority of the Scriptures themselves in all matters of faith. And that is why we must ever insist upon that vital matter. There are those who say that they do not accept the authority of the Scriptures but that they believe in the Lord Jesus Christ. The question I ask is, how do they know Him? What do they know about the Lord Jesus Christ except what they find in the New Testament?

It is there, it seems to me, that this whole so-called higher critical approach to the Scriptures is, in the last analysis, not merely an error but utter folly. How can I sit in judgment on the New Testament? How can I say *this* is true of Christ, but *that* is not? What do I know about Christ apart from the New Testament? I am shut up to this Book; anything that I may say that I believe apart from the Bible will be sheer imagination. That is why this talk about going directly to Christ (without reference to the Scriptures) is, according to the New Testament, the most dangerous position one can be in. That is why the New Testament epistles were written, to correct error and heresy. 'Believe,' says John in this chapter, 'not every spirit, but try the spirits whether they are of God: because many false prophets are gone out into the world. Hereby know ye the Spirit of God: every spirit that confesseth that Jesus Christ is come in the flesh is of God' (vv. 1-2).

In those first years there were all sorts of apocryphal gospels. There were men drawing on their imagination, and, perhaps inspired by the devil himself, they were spreading stories about the teachings of Jesus of Nazareth and were making havoc in the life of the early church. So God raised up the Apostles to write these authoritative accounts, in order that we might know what is true and what is false; that is the whole purpose of our belief in the canon of Scripture. The promise of Jesus Christ to the disciples when He said the Holy Spirit would guide them into all truth was fulfilled in the writing of the New Testament Scriptures; and the wisdom given to the Church to deliver the canon of Scripture is that which can be traced back to the Apostles and which therefore can be regarded as the Word of God. And John, in a sense, is just saying at this particular point that if we do make this confession that Jesus is the Son of God, then God dwells in us and we in God; we can only make that statement because of those people who have seen and testified that 'the Father has sent the Son to be the Saviour of the world.'

Let me again, therefore, stress and emphasise that the second great principle is that a correct belief means the acceptance of and agreement with the apostolic witness and testimony. I know no Christ apart from the Christ I find in the New Testament. I have no immediacy or directness of approach. I do not believe in visions, and I cannot find Christ directly; I find Him in the Scriptures. That was the great emphasis of the Protestant Reformation, and we must come back to it. A lot of mystical talk is made in an attempt to avoid the authority of Scripture because of its miraculous and supernatural element. People have been reconstructing a Jesus of their own, but he is not the Jesus of the New Testament. Which Jesus can I know apart from *this* Jesus? I am, therefore, shut up to the Bible, and I either accept the apostolic witness and teaching or I reject it. I ask again, how can people living in the twentieth century sit in judgment upon the Gospels? What do they know? By what canon do they describe and define this Jesus they depict? I know nothing about Him apart from what I am told concerning Him in the Bible, which is the record and the account of the apostolic witness and the apostolic testimony.

Ah, let us be careful of these subtle temptations of Satan which would try to persuade us that we are in a superior spiritual condition! I once read an article in which a man claimed that those of us who believe in the ultimate authority of Scripture and who bank our all upon it are guilty of what he calls seeing the Book rather than the Saviour. He claims he is in a superior spiritual condition, and this is the position taken up at the present time by those who claim that their authority is Christ. 'We do not see the Book,' they say; 'Christ himself is the authority.' To which again I ask my question: What do you know about Christ apart from the Book? Who is your Christ unless He conforms to this? Who is the Christ who gives you the authority? The Bible—that is my authority. I am dependent upon the record and witness of John the Baptist—of Peter, James, and John and the other disciples and Apostles who preached and bore testimony to these first Christians.

And that brings me to my third great principle: What is this correct belief? Now here we are outside the realm of controversy if we accept the apostolic witness and testimony and we remind ourselves of the very centralities of our faith. We have been looking at the mountain range; now let us centre on this glorious peak that stretches up to heaven and beyond them all. What is it? 'We have seen and do testify that the Father sent the Son to be the Saviour of the world.'

I see the importance of the apostolic witness. What is it? John, in effect, is putting it like this: 'The important thing is to know God. But how can I know God? "No man hath seen God at any time." But we have seen and do testify that Jesus is the Son of God.' That is the statement. Notice how he puts it. He had not had a vision. What then? Thank God, 'we *have seen*.' He said it all in the introduction: 'That which . . . we have seen with our eyes, which we have looked upon, and our hands have handled, of the Word of life . . . that which we have seen and heard we declare unto you,' said John. 'No man hath seen God, but we have seen Jesus, and Jesus said, "He that hath seen me hath seen the Father"' (see John 14:9).

In other words, the apostolic vision on which my faith is grounded is this: It is a belief in that which the Apostles tell us they saw, and the explanation of their understanding of what they saw is found in the four Gospels. The statements in the Gospels are not simply objective statements; they are statements plus interpretation, and at long last modern man has come back to see that. They used to contrast John with Matthew, Mark, and Luke. They said that John preached, but that Matthew, Mark, and Luke just gave the facts. But they now have to admit that what they wrote was facts plus interpretation. Like John, the men who wrote the first three Gospels believed and understood that Jesus is the Son of God and the Saviour of the world. They saw and they testified; in other words, they saw and they expounded.

What, then, did they see, and what did they expound? There were two elements, a double emphasis. The first statement is that Jesus is the Son of God. 'We have seen,' says John. This word 'seen' is a strong word; it means 'gazed upon.' He used that same word in the prologue of his Gospel—'and we beheld his glory' (John 1:14). To behold is not merely to give a cursory glance; it is not a passing glimpse of something. No; we have looked upon, we have beheld, we have sat in amazement, we have contemplated, we have seen, 'and we beheld his glory, the glory as of the only begotten of the Father, full of grace and truth.' That is it!

What John is saying is something like this: 'We looked at His person, and I remember the enigma that was presented to us. We looked at Him. He was a man like every other man apparently, and He had worked as a carpenter. He was quite ordinary, and yet He was always surprising us. There was something—a radiance—a glory that kept on peeping out. There was something unearthly, and we said one to another, "What is it?" He frightened us at times, this ordinary person who became extraordinary suddenly—there was something about Him. "We beheld His glory." And then there were His teachings. He had never been to the schools; He had never had any learning in a formal sense, and yet He taught as one having authority, and not as the Scribes. And there was the way in which He handled the Doctors of the Law. There was the sermon He preached one day on a mountain with those extraordinary Beatitudes of His. There was a glory that came out in His words; gracious words came streaming forth from His lips.

'And then there were His works—the things which we saw Him do. We were in a boat with Him one day, and He was asleep in the stern of the vessel when suddenly a storm arose, and the water was gradually filling up our little boat, and we were trying to get rid of it, but we could do nothing. We felt we would be drowned at any moment, and we awoke Him and said, "Master, we perish," and what did He do but rebuke the waves and they were still, and we were afraid. And on another occasion we saw Him even raise a man who was dead. A poor widow came out of a town called Nain mourning her dead son. We were going into the town, and we met, and He spoke a word, and the dead arose. And we remember, too, what happened in Jairus' house. He mastered the elements; He controlled everything—life, death, all things seemed subservient to His supernatural power—His works, His miracles. We beheld the glory streaming and shining out of it all. He did signs and wonders, and they proclaimed to us that He was the Son of God.

'But we also saw things happening to Him. I remember,' says John, 'how one day he told Peter and James and myself to come aside with Him. He said, "I want to take you three to the top of that mountain; we will leave the others for a time. I want you three alone to be with Me." So we went to the top of the mountain, and there we saw His whole body transformed and transfigured. It became shining and exceedingly white, and we saw two men appearing. They were Elijah and Moses, and they talked; and then we heard a voice from heaven—we beheld His glory—and the voice said, "This is my beloved Son, in whom I am well pleased; hear Him." It was the transfiguration!

'And I remember seeing Him in the Garden, sweating drops of blood. And I remember looking at Him upon the cross, and the words He spoke to me there—and we beheld His glory. We saw Him buried, yes, but He appeared to us afterwards. We saw Him resurrected, and He came and spoke to us. He came into the room with the door shut, and on another occasion He sat down and ate some broiled fish with us. We have seen, and we testify—we beheld His glory. Indeed, we were with Him one day, and suddenly we saw Him rising and ascending into the clouds and into heaven, and He disappeared out of our sight. We believe, we have seen, and we do testify. And then we remember that amazing day at Pentecost at Jerusalem when He promised that the Holy Ghost would come upon us, and we began to speak with strange, new tongues, and we were filled with power and radiance ourselves—we have seen and we do testify.'

That is the record. So, I say, what makes men and women Christians is that they confess that. They do not merely accept it intellectually. They say, 'This is the thing that matters; this is the thing by which I live; this is the thing which means life to me.' They confess that Jesus is the Son of God.

Ah yes, but they also confess that He is 'the Saviour of the world.' In other words, these men taught and reminded people of what Jesus Himself had been saying. They reminded the people of how He once said, 'The Son of Man came not to be ministered unto, but to minister, and to give his life a ransom for many' (Matt 20:28). They remembered the word of John the Baptist: 'Behold the Lamb of God, which taketh away the sin of the world!' (John 1:29). They remembered that He said, 'I must go to Jerusalem' and that He set His face steadfastly to go there—there was this compulsion, this constraint. They remembered how He himself had said, 'For this cause came I unto this hour. . . . And I, if I be lifted up from the earth, will draw all men unto me' (John 12:27, 32). They remembered all this, and they taught it.

That was the apostolic teaching and witness and testimony. They did not go around preaching moral uplift or talking about the international situation. They gave these facts about this extraordinary person that they had seen. They said, 'This is the Son of God; this is what happened to Him, and the meaning of it all is that He has been sent by God to be the Saviour of the world.' That was their preaching! They said in effect, 'We did not understand Him fully until after the resurrection. There seemed to us to be a strange contradiction in Him; He made these exalted claims, and yet He appeared to be so weak. He said He could do everything. He could raise the dead, but He could not save Himself on the cross. So we were very dejected when He was buried in the grave; but then He rose again, and He came back and spoke to us. He opened the Scriptures to us; He took us through the Old Testament, and He showed us that the Christ had to suffer. He expounded the doctrine of the atonement to us. He said, "I am the Lamb of God. My Father has placed the sins of the world upon Me. I have died to set you free." He opened our understanding of the Scriptures.'

That was the Apostles' preaching that was the apostolic witness and testimony. Jesus—who He is, what He means, the explanation of His extraordinary life and death, His rising again and ascension, and ultimately what it all means to us—can be put in this form. Whoever confesses that Jesus is the Son of God is one who has come to understand God's great love to us, which is the theme of John's next statement in verse 16. The Apostles really were teaching the love of God, that 'God so loved the world, that he gave his only begotten Son, that whosoever believeth in him should not perish, but have everlasting life' (John 3:16). They perish apart from Him; but believing on Him, they do not perish but have everlasting life. 'Whosoever shall confess,' therefore, that 'Jesus is the Son of God' has accepted the Apostles' teaching.

You see, that includes it all—not only the doctrine of the Incarnation, not merely the teaching, not only the miracles, but the death, the meaning of the death, the whole idea of the atonement; that He is 'the Saviour of the world'—God's way of salvation. Those who believe that, says John, can be quite certain that God dwells in them and they in God, for apart from this indwelling of the Holy Spirit, Jesus of Nazareth is but a man—a political agitator to some, a moral exemplar to others, just a philosopher to others, the pale Galilean to another. People do not understand that the princes of the world look at Him, but they never behold His glory. But these men, the Apostles, 'beheld His glory, the glory as of the only begotten of the Father,' and we have their record and witness and testimony; and if I accept and see it and give my assent to it from my heart, there is only one reason why I do so, and that is that the Holy Spirit has opened my eyes. I can thus say, 'I know that God dwells in me and I in God.' It is the Spirit who 'searcheth all things, yea, the deep things of God' (1 Cor 2:10). God opens blind eyes; however poor and weak and ignorant we may be, He can enable us to behold Him with the eye of faith.

And so I accept the record, I subscribe to the testimony, and through their eyes, as it were, I behold His glory, 'the glory as of the only begotten of the Father, full of grace and truth.' I therefore say that 'the Father sent the Son to be the Saviour of the world' and to be *my* Saviour.

10
The Saviour

> And we have seen and do testify that the Father sent the Son to be the Saviour of the world.
>
> 1 JOHN 4:14

We return once more to this great statement which I have compared to a great mountain peak. I feel, with this fourteenth verse, very much as Peter, I imagine, must have felt when on the Mountain of Transfiguration with James and John. They had been taken up by our Lord, and when Moses and Elijah appeared, Peter said, 'Let us make here three tabernacles; one for thee, and one for Moses, and one for Elijah' (Matt 17:4). In other words, the glory had so gripped him that he said, 'Let us stay here.' This glory was so very different from the world down in the plain, and as I read this verse, I think I understand him.

We are concerned about the whole argument of the Apostle, and the argument is vital if our Christian experience is to be a triumphant and victorious one. Yet, though we are concerned about the argument, I find it difficult to leave this peak, this glorious height represented in this verse. Indeed, I can justify our return to it in this way: If we are not perfectly happy about the statement of this verse, then the argument completely collapses, because it is based upon this statement. So there is a sense in which we must stay on this mountain a little longer. All the argument that is deduced by the Apostle is deduced from this fundamental postulate, so that if there is any suspicion of doubt, or even the faintest query in our minds about it, we cannot work out the Christian faith, and we have no grounds of assurance and confidence. Therefore, we come back and look at it again.

This is the statement: 'We have seen and do testify that the Father sent the Son to be the Saviour of the world.' The whole of the gospel in a phrase! This is the only time in which John uses the expression 'Saviour' in the entire epistle. He gives the same teaching, of course, in other places. We have already had it back at the beginning, in the second chapter,[1] where he says that our Lord is 'the propitiation for our sins: and not for ours only, but also for the sins of the whole world' (v 2). There is a sense in which he repeats the saying here, but he does not use this precise phrase and describe Him as 'the Saviour of the world' except at this point. To those who are interested in these matters, which are more or less mechanical and yet have their place, it is interesting to observe that John only twice in the whole of his writings uses this phrase. You find it again in John 4 in connection with the woman of Samaria, but it is not a characteristic of his writings. Paul, however, is fond of it, and if you examine his epistles, you will find that he often makes use of this particular expression.

Another important thing is to be certain that we grasp the meaning. Earlier we looked at it in this way: We looked at the person of our Lord—we considered the apostolic witness and testimony with regard to the person, the emphasis being that Jesus is the Son of God; and that, of course, is logically the statement which must come first. The essential doctrine concerning Jesus of Nazareth is always this two-fold doctrine: His person and His work; and there is a sense in which we simply cannot understand the work and the nature of the work until we are perfectly clear in our minds with regard to the person Himself. And so, having looked at the person, we now go forward and are proposing to look at the work which is done by the person—'We have seen and do testify that the Father sent the Son to be the Saviour of the world.'

All I want to do here is to underline some of the essential things which are conveyed by this magnificent and glorious statement of the gospel. In other words, we must look at this word 'Saviour.' What does it mean exactly? It is very important that one should ask a question like that, because one of the great difficulties in connection with theology and Christian thought, especially in this present century, has been that men and women have persisted in using Christian terminology, but have emptied it of the real meaning and have imposed their own. There are people who talk of Christ as Saviour, but they certainly do not mean by that what the New Testament means.

Let me illustrate this. The word 'Saviour' does not merely mean a helper. We are not told that the Father sent the Son to help mankind; it does not mean that He is just someone who assists. Nor does it mean that He is just one who teaches or indicates to us what we ought to do; He is not merely an instructor. Indeed, I would go further and say that the term 'Saviour' and its connotation must not be thought of in terms of an example or pattern or encourager. I use these various terms because so often people speak about our Lord as 'Saviour,' and yet if you ask them to define what they mean by it, they will tell you something of that kind. Their conception of Christ as Saviour can be put like this: He saves us by preaching the Sermon on the Mount and by describing a certain kind of life. He does this by setting before us a great example—as one who lived that high and exalted teaching; and He is constantly calling us to rise to the same height. They say that Christ as Saviour is one who is marching ahead of us and who is leading the way, turning around occasionally to appeal to us and to inspire us to follow in His footsteps, so that ultimately we shall succeed in scaling the heights with Him and will arrive in the presence of God.

Now the element that is seen in all those ideas is this: that ultimately it is you and I who have to save ourselves, and what the

Lord does is to aid and assist us—to give us encouragement and make it somewhat easier for us to do so. Now that, of course, is clearly a complete denial not only of the Biblical teaching, but also of the historic faith and creeds of the Christian Church. To use the term *Saviour* with regard to our Lord and mean something like that is dishonest, for it takes the original meaning right out and substitutes for it something that is utterly foreign to the New Testament.

Perhaps the best way to put that is this: If that is all that is meant by 'Saviour,' then Jesus of Nazareth is no Saviour at all. That is something that had already been tried, and it had failed before He ever came into this world. God confronted the children of Israel and gave them the Ten Commandments and the moral law. He said to them, 'Ye shall therefore keep my statutes, and my judgements: which if a man do, he shall live in them' (Lev 18:5). That was God's challenge, as it were, in the giving of the law to the children of Israel, and the whole story of the Old Testament shows us that men and women failed, and failed entirely. 'There is none righteous, no, not one'; 'all have sinned, and come short of the glory of God'; '... that every mouth may be stopped, and all the world may become guilty before God' (Rom. 3:10, 23, 19). That describes the world as the result of trying to save itself by keeping the law and the commandments of God. That is a complete failure. There was not a character in the Old Testament who did not fail. The greatest prophets failed and were conscious of sin; the greatest saints were all defeated by sin and by Satan.

I repeat, therefore, that if our Lord and Saviour is to be the Saviour on some such terms, then all He does is really to make things quite impossible for us. For if I cannot keep the Ten Commandments and the moral law, what is the point in confronting me with the Sermon on the Mount? If I cannot even satisfy my own demands, if I cannot come up to the standard of the saints, what is the point of putting before me Jesus of Nazareth? He makes it utterly impossible for me! I, for myself, have never been able to understand the mentality of people who can glibly talk about 'the imitation of Christ' and who believe that they are meant to save themselves and that our Lord just helps them in this external way by giving them a kind of general encouragement. I know of nothing more discouraging than the life of Jesus Christ, taken in that way! If I am left to myself I am entirely undone, I am damned before I move, I am utterly hopeless.

But that is a complete misinterpretation and misrepresentation of what is meant by the phrase 'the Saviour of the world.' Surely the whole Biblical meaning of this particular term should rather be put like this: Christ is the Saviour as the result of something that He has done. We must get rid once and for ever of this idea that we are the actors and receive encouragement from Him. Not at all! The Biblical representation is that God sent Him into the world to do something, and that we are saved as the result of something He has done quite apart from ourselves and our own action. He has acted, and it is His action that produces salvation and the way of escape for us.

Now here is something that is utterly fundamental and primary, and unless we are agreed with this statement there is really no point or purpose in our proceeding any further. Salvation, according to the New Testament—take, for instance, Colossians 1 where you have a perfect illustration of salvation—is something that is entirely worked out by the Lord Jesus Christ. It is something that has come to men and women as a free gift to them, and they have nothing to do but to receive this gift. It is something provided; it is the righteousness of God which is given.

That is something which is surely basic, and of course there is no phrase, perhaps, that puts all this more perfectly than that great and glorious phrase which was uttered by our Lord Himself upon the cross when He cried out, 'It is finished' (John 19:30). He had already talked about having to finish the work which the Father had sent Him to do. He spoke as one who had been given a particular task, and He set out upon it, and there, with His last breath as it were, He cried out, 'I have done it! I have completed the work which Thou gavest Me to do.' Christ is the Saviour; we do not save ourselves. It is He who saves, and our salvation arises from Him and is derived from something He has done once and for ever on our behalf. 'The Father sent the Son to be the Saviour of the world.'

Of course, if you read the Book of Acts you will find that the Apostles and the first preachers went around the world, and this is exactly what they preached. They said that they had great, good news to offer to the people; they were making an announcement, as the angels had already made the announcement to the shepherds. They went from place to place, and they said in effect, 'We are bearers of glad tidings; we have something to tell you, and what we tell you is that God in His Son has done something which means salvation and deliverance for the world.' So that is the first thing we have to realise, that He is 'the Saviour' and that salvation is something that is worked out by Him.

Having said that, having seen that He Himself, by what He does, is the Saviour, let us briefly consider the second principle: how the Lord Jesus Christ saves us. We have already seen that He is the Son of God, that He is the one who has come, who has been sent into the world. He is not an ordinary man born like others; He has been sent from heaven, He has come into the world. So how does He save? I can merely give you a summary of what the Bible teaches in this respect.

First of all, we are told that He saves us by His life of perfect obedience to God's holy law. So the life of Jesus Christ has its importance in that way and in that respect. When we talk about salvation, we have to realise our predicament and our position, and here it is: God has given the law to mankind, and He has told all people that they must keep the law. God has said that if they do not do so, they will be punished, and the punishment is death. God's law stands, and it can never be uprooted. It is eternal; it is an expression of the character of God Himself, and before anyone can be saved, that law of God has to be fulfilled—it has to be honoured and satisfied. That was, therefore, the first task confronting our

Lord Jesus Christ. No one had ever succeeded or could ever succeed in keeping the law, and that law must be kept; so the first thing He did was to live a life of absolute obedience to it. In all things He fulfilled righteousness; every demand of the law positively was answered and was satisfied by His blameless, spotless life.

But, of course, that is not the end. For the law not only makes its positive demands on us—it pronounces its judgment upon us, and it has already pronounced that judgment: 'the wages of sin is death' (Rom 6:23). Those who fail to keep the law know that they are under the wrath of God, and the punishment meted out by God for this failure is death; so they are confronted with that positive enactment. Therefore the second thing that our Lord has to do is to deal with this problem of the guilt of man face-to-face with the law of God, and according to the Scriptures He has done so once and for ever by going to His cruel death upon the cross on Calvary's hill.

We are always confronted by the cross; we cannot get away from it. It is central in the New Testament. Look at all the wealth of detail we are told about it in the four Gospels; look at the emphasis placed upon it in the Acts and in the epistles. It is there always— for example, 'in whom we have redemption through his blood' (Eph 1:7). You cannot get away from this blood in the New Testament. It is central; without it there is no salvation. The law of God demands sin's punishment, and the punishment is death; so our Lord came face-to-face with that demand likewise. Before He could be 'the Saviour of the world,' He had to satisfy the demands that the law makes upon guilty sinners in the sight of God. The message is that He went to the Cross; He set His face steadfastly to go to Jerusalem; He would not be delivered. He told His servants in effect, 'I could command twelve legions of angels; but if I did, how could I fulfill all righteousness? I must meet the demands of the law.' He gave Himself as an offering and a sacrifice; He died passively there upon the cross, and God poured upon Him His wrath against the sin of man. He is our Saviour by His atoning death as well as by His perfect, blameless, spotless life of obedience.

But even that does not exhaust this idea of Christ as our Saviour, for you will find that the author of the Epistle to the Hebrews takes us beyond that. He tells us that our Lord has become the great High Priest. There on the cross He was the sacrifice and the offering, and He is also the High Priest. The writer says that He entered into heaven by His own blood. 'Neither by the blood of goats and calves, but by his own blood he entered in once into the holy place, having obtained eternal redemption for us' (Heb 9:12). By His own precious blood which was shed upon the cross He there demanded, as it were, the release of the captives, the setting free of the guilty, the absolution of the sins of man. And because of the work that He has done there upon the cross, He has entered into heaven.

But He does not stop at that either, for we are told that He is seated at the right hand of God and that He is there interceding on our behalf, and that is why He is able to save to the uttermost those that come unto God by Him (Heb 7:25). He is there, and His very presence is pleading the merit of His blood. John has already put that like this: 'If any man sin, we have an advocate with the Father, Jesus Christ the righteous' (2:1). He is there advocating our cause by His presence, interceding on our behalf with God. He is not trying to persuade an unwilling God to look upon us and to forgive us and have mercy upon us, for as John tells us, it was the Father Himself who 'sent the Son to be the Saviour of the world.' He there, by His very presence, guarantees that we are forgiven, and He there, as it were, is offering His blood, and it is in this way that God forgives us.

But there is even more! We are told that it is only thus, in a sense, that we can pray to God. Our prayers are taken by our Lord, and He offers them up to the Father. He adds the incense of His own holiness; He takes our unworthy prayers and petitions, and He transmutes them with His own perfection and presents them to the

Father, so that in all these actions He is the Saviour, He is acting as our Saviour, He is representing us before God. And thus, in Him God looks upon us and absolves us from all our guilt.

But according to the New Testament, this idea of *Saviour* is even richer than that. For He not only saves us by the objective work which He does in the way I have been trying to describe, but He saves us also by coming to dwell in us by His Holy Spirit. Here, of course, we are again directly looking at these magnificent statements that are made by John in this section of the epistle. God dwells in us, and we in him. He has already said that He has given us His Holy Spirit; and by entering into our lives by the Holy Spirit, our Lord is carrying on this work of saving our souls, for not only do we need thus to be represented in the presence of God and to be justified by the law before we can stand in the presence of God and dwell with God for all eternity, but we also need to be perfected, to be cleansed and purified. So our Lord Jesus Christ, we are told, enters within us and dwells within us and works within us 'both to will and to do of his good pleasure' (Phil 2:13).

And then the last step in this mighty work which our Lord does as our Saviour is the work that yet remains for Him to do. While on earth He kept the law and died for us; then He ascended into heaven and presented His offering. He is seated there, and He intercedes and acts as an advocate for us. He enters into us and works within us, and yet even there the work is not finished. There is still something final that remains to be done, and Paul in writing to the Philippians puts it like this: 'Our conversation [our citizenship],' he says, 'is in heaven,' and then he adds, 'from whence also we look for the Saviour, the Lord Jesus Christ: who shall change our vile body [our body of humiliation], that it may be fashioned like unto his glorious body, according to the working whereby he is able even to subdue all things unto himself' (Phil 3:20-21).

What he means by that, of course, is that before our salvation is complete, our very bodies have to be redeemed and glorified and changed and saved. And the announcement of the New Testament is that Christ as Saviour will again come into this world; and when He does so, in that great regeneration He will take us and our very bodies and will then form and fashion them according to His mighty working, in order that we may be perfect and complete, saved in body, soul, and spirit, and we shall be faultless and blameless in the presence of God.

We have thus hurried through these great aspects of the work of our Lord and Saviour Jesus Christ—the Saviour of our souls. But perhaps the best way to look at it is for me to give you a summary of what it is that He saves us from. For this idea of salvation of necessity carries this need of being saved *from* something, and that can be put like this:

Our Lord and Saviour Jesus Christ clearly saves us, in the first instance, from the guilt and the penalty of sin. We are all, as we have seen, guilty before God and before His holy law. We are guilty in His presence; so the first thing I need is to be saved from the guilt of my sin. I need a Saviour in that respect apart from anything else. I have broken the law of God, and I am under the condemnation of that holy law; so before I can talk about salvation or about being saved, I must be perfectly clear that I am delivered from the guilt of my sin. That is the glorious message that the New Testament Gospel brings to me. In Christ my guilt is removed. It is no use my facing the future and proposing to live a better life; I am confronted by my own past—I cannot avoid it, I cannot escape it. I have broken the law—I must deal with the problem of my guilt—and I cannot do so. I cannot undo my past; I cannot make atonement for my misdeeds and for everything I have done against God. I must be delivered from the guilt of my sin, and Christ—and Christ alone—can so deliver me.

But having thus had the assurance that the guilt of my sin has been dealt with, I am still confronted by the power of sin. The world in which I live is against me; it does not encourage me to live a Christian life. I battle the world and the flesh and the devil; forces and factors outside me are trying to drag me down, and I am aware of their terrible power. The man or woman who has not realised the power of sin all around him or her is a novice in these matters. The whole outlook of the world, the whole of its pleasures and organisations—the whole mentality of the modern world—is something that is opposed to my highest interest. If you consult the Bible, you will find that no man can deliver himself from this power. As I have already reminded you, the prophets and the patriarchs and the greatest saints have all failed. God's people throughout the centuries have testified to this terrible malign power that is opposing them in the world, and they cannot conquer it. There is only one who has conquered Satan, there is only one who has conquered and defeated the world, and that is this Son whom the Father sent into the world to be its Saviour. Jesus Christ can deliver me from the *power* of sin as well as from the *guilt* of sin.

The third and last thing He delivers me from is what the Fathers used to call the 'pollution' of sin. I am not only confronted by sin all around me, but there is sin within me. The Apostle Paul said he had discovered that 'in me (that is, in my flesh,) dwelleth no good thing' (Rom 7:18). My very nature is polluted; there is a desire for and an inclination towards evil. Apart from my actions, my *nature* is sinful, and that is where all the sinless perfectionists who think of sin only in terms of actions go so sadly and hopelessly astray. Before I do anything, my nature is polluted; there is a sinful propensity in me, and I need to be delivered from that. I need to be saved from it; and, blessed be the name of God, according to the Scriptures the Lord Jesus Christ as Saviour deals with that problem also! He not only saves from the guilt of sin and the power of sin but also from this terrible pollution of sin, and that is the special work of the Holy Spirit within us. He deals with us; He reveals sin to us; He creates a hatred of sin. He shows the enormity of sin; He gives a desire for holiness; He encourages us to engage in good works. He is working within us, for He has been sent by the Son, the Saviour, thus to perfect, to purify, and to cleanse us, and to rid us of this foul pollution of sin. And the result of this work ultimately will be that He will present us faultless and blameless without spot and without rebuke, without any vestige of pollution in the presence of God in glory.

That, in its essence, is what the New Testament would teach us concerning the Lord Jesus Christ as the Saviour of our souls. You can see that He is not a helper, nor is He an assistant. He is not merely one who encourages us; He is not only an example to follow. How can I follow? He is so glorious, so holy and divine, that I cannot. And thank God that I am not called upon to do so, in that way! Primarily, this is the message: He is the Saviour, He has kept the law, He has satisfied its demands, and He offers me His righteousness. He is working in me mightily, as Paul puts it, in order to deliver me from sin in all its aspects, and eventually He will take me by the hand and will present me to His Father, and I shall be received into everlasting glory.

'We have seen and do testify that the Father sent the Son' in order that He might be 'the Saviour of the world.'

So the question we ask ourselves is this: Do I realise that Christ is my Saviour in that way? Do I believe that He is the Son of God and the Saviour of my soul? On what am I relying as I think of facing God? Do I look to my own life and actions, or do I look entirely to Christ–Christ as 'Saviour'? I either depend upon Him or I depend upon myself; but He and He alone is the Saviour of my soul.

11

Knowing the Love of God

> And we have known and believed the love that God hath to us. God is love; and he that dwelleth in love dwelleth in God, and God in him.
>
> 1 JOHN 4:16

In this verse, the Apostle sums up what he has been saying and arguing. First of all, this is the summing up of what he has just been saying in the immediately preceding context; he both sums it up and carries it a stage further. He has been reminding us that he and the other Apostles 'have seen and do testify that the Father sent the Son to be the Saviour of the world'; then he says, 'Whosoever shall confess that Jesus is the Son of God . . .' In other words, he puts his signature to what he has testified. 'Whosoever,' he says in effect, 'says, "amen" to what we have testified and witnessed can be sure that God dwells in him and he in God. So then,' John says, 'we [no longer merely himself and the Apostles, but all Christians] have known and believed the love–of which I have been speaking–the love that God has for us.' This is a summing up of the immediate context; he takes it beyond the state of belief to that of knowledge.

In a sense, John is dealing here partly with the relationship between belief and experience, and it seems to me that there are two main suggestions at this point. The first is the vital importance of our understanding something of the connection between the objective and the subjective in the realm of our Christian life. This is the special glory of our Christian position—that it is at one and the same time objective and subjective. It is outside us, and it is inside us; it is something which is believed as a body of truth, of doctrine, or of dogma; and yet it is experimental. It is life, it is actual, it is living.

Now here is a very vital and important subject. The history of the church and the history of God's people throughout the centuries in every country shows forcibly that much harm and trouble is often caused by a failure to regard the relationship between the objective and the subjective in the way in which the New Testament itself does. There seems to be this fatal tendency in all of us as a result of sin and the Fall to concentrate exclusively on either the one or the other. There are those who are interested in theology and doctrine in a purely intellectual sense. It is full of great beauty and truth, which they are interested in, but they are not always concerned with practise. They will sometimes lose their tempers with one another as they talk about the love of God, thereby showing that it is purely theoretical, something entirely in the mind which has never been applied and translated into life and has never been experienced.

On the other hand, there are those to whom the Christian life is purely subjective, and they dismiss dogma. They are not interested; they are not concerned about definitions; they say the only thing that matters is that we should be able to say, 'Whereas once I was like that, now I am like this.' 'Don't talk to me about your doctrine,' they say, 'I have had an experience—I have felt something.' The tragedy is that we should ever be guilty of one or the other; furthermore, it seems to me that one is as bad as the other, for the glory of the gospel is that it always takes up the whole man—not only the mind, not only the heart, not only the will, but mind, heart, and will. Paul puts this in a resounding statement when he says, 'But ye have obeyed from the heart that form of doctrine which was delivered you' (Rom 6:17). They obeyed with their will, they obeyed from the heart—there is the emotion. And what had they obeyed?—the form of sound words of doctrine that was delivered to them; there is an objective statement of the truth that comes to the mind.

Here in this particular section John puts this all very plainly and clearly to us. You see, he does not talk about what we know and believe until he has first of all put it in the objective form. He says, 'We, the apostles, have seen and do testify'; there is the message. But what am I to believe, what am I to know, what am I to experience? That which has already been testified by the Apostles. In other words, we must always be sure and certain that we follow the order as it is laid here and everywhere else in Scripture. The love of God is only known and felt adequately and completely in and through our Lord and Saviour Jesus Christ.

John has gone on repeating this, and you notice how he never tires of doing so. 'In this was manifested the love of God toward us, because that God sent his only begotten Son into the world, that we might live through him' (v 9); and, 'We have seen and do testify that the Father sent the Son' (v 14). He repeats it again. This is because he knew that in his own day and age there were all those so-called mystery religions or curious cults which talked about the love of God; and they all tried to teach that you can know the love of God directly. That is always the characteristic of mysticism; what finally condemns mysticism is that it bypasses the Lord Jesus Christ. Anything that bypasses Christ is not Christian. I do not care what it is, however good, however uplifting or noble; it is Christ who is the manifestation of the love of God, says John.

I do not hesitate, therefore, to aver and to add as strongly as follows: I must distrust any emotion that I may have within me with respect to God unless it is based solidly upon the Lord Jesus Christ. In Him God has manifested His love. 'God commendeth his love toward us, in that, while we were yet sinners, Christ died for us' (Rom 5:8). Therefore, I say that I must never attempt by any means or method to get to know God or to to try to make myself love God except in and through my Lord and Saviour Jesus Christ. I must avoid every other direct approach to God, every direct dealing with God. There is but 'one mediator between God and men, the man Christ Jesus' (1 Tim 2:5), and without Him I have no knowledge of God. So any love which is not based upon this is to be distrusted. And in the same way I would argue that a belief which does not lead to such a love is in and of itself useless.

Let us, then, leave it at that. But let us always remember the objective and the subjective; the objective is the doctrine concerning the Lord Jesus Christ, and if I truly believe that, then I will love. Let me put it again in a phrase from the Apostle Peter: 'Unto you therefore which believe he is precious' (1 Pet 2:7). There is little value in confession unless He becomes precious to us. 'We have known and believed the love that God hath to us'; I have not only believed, I *know* it.

That takes me to my second point—the relationship between knowledge and faith. It is a great subject, and let me first just make one or two remarks in passing.

The first is that there is a sense in which knowledge and belief always go together and must go together. There is a sense in which we can argue that you cannot believe a thing unless you know it. It is an old and a great question as to which comes first: belief or knowledge. Indeed, there is a sense in which it is a foolish question. You must have a certain amount of knowledge of what you believe. You believe something, and if you do, then you know what you believe, and that is knowledge. So there is a sense in which a person who believes, knows. You do not believe in a vacuum; nor do you believe something vague and nebulous. You believe something, and that defines it and makes it concrete.

But, of course, there is another sense, looking at it from the experimental standpoint, in which knowledge is something that always follows. As Browning put it, 'A man's reach should always be greater than his grasp.' So in that sense I think the New Testament does teach very clearly that our knowledge always follows our belief. It is like a horse drawing a carriage; they are bound together, and they are never separated, but the horse is always in front, and the carriage is being drawn by him. Belief, then knowledge—that is the position. The Apostle Paul states the whole thing in Philippians 3. He thanks God for the knowledge that he has in Christ Jesus his Lord, and yet he goes on to say, 'that I may know him' (Phil 3:10). He forgets the things that are behind and presses forward towards the mark. Nevertheless, 'whereto we have already attained . . . let us mind the same thing' (v 16). We know certain things, and yet we want to know more; knowledge follows belief and is always being led onwards by it.

In other words, we may put it like this perhaps, that knowledge is but a more sure form of belief. Knowledge is that state in which I really have grasped what I have believed. I possess it perfectly; in a sense I knew it at the beginning, but what I believed, I have now really got. John is here emphasising the certainty of belief. He says in effect, 'We know and have believed the love that God has towards us.' It is as if he were saying, 'Thank God, you and I who are Christians—we know this love of God; and yet we do not know it all yet. It is too big—it is so high—it is so broad and deep. We will join all the saints in investigating it. Thank God, we know, and yet we do not know! We will go on to know; we will go on increasing in knowledge.'

That is why John puts knowledge before belief: I do not know, and yet I know much more than I have actually experienced. I have experienced, yes, but my belief is greater than my experience, and I am stretching forward unto that which I have not yet attained. So there is nothing odd about putting knowledge before belief. I think it is a very good way of putting it. I have, and yet I want; I possess, and yet there is more to be possessed. The love of God is like a mighty ocean; I am swimming in it, and yet how much remains!

We know, and we have believed, and we ever go on, therefore, to know more perfectly that which we believe by faith.

Therefore, it seems to me that the great thing here is that we come to the practical application of all this. John is summing up. He has finished with arguments and propositions, and now he comes back to this experimental aspect. So the great question is whether we can join John and the first Christians in saying that we know this love of God to us. After all, there is little value in our profession unless it lead to some practical result in our lives. John was writing to men and women in a difficult world, even as we are in a difficult world; and the thrilling thing, he tells them, is that although the whole world lies under the power of the evil one, it is possible for our joy to abound.

How can my joy abound? How can I walk through this world with my head erect? How can I come through triumphantly? Well, here is the main thing: I should know this love which God has towards me. If I have that, I can say that 'neither death, nor life . . . nor height, nor depth, nor any other creature, shall be able to separate us from the love of God, which is in Christ Jesus our Lord' (Rom 8:38-39). Therefore, the questions come to us one by one: Do I know this love? Can I make this statement? It is made everywhere in the New Testament. Paul is fond of stating it generally, and yet you find that he also delights in stating it particularly: '. . . the Son of God, who loved me, and gave himself for me' (Gal 2:20). No man could state the doctrine of the atonement in all its plenitude and glory like the Apostle Paul, and yet here he says, He died for me; He loved me. This is personal knowledge, personal appropriation. You find this everywhere in the New Testament. For example, 'Whom having not seen,' says Peter, 'ye love; in whom, though now ye see him not, yet believing, ye rejoice with joy unspeakable and full of glory' (1 Pet 1:8).

Do we do that? These people did not see Him, and so we cannot argue and say, 'It is all very well for those first Christians; they saw Him. If only I could see Christ, then I would love Him.' But they did not see Him any more than we see Him. They had the apostolic witness and teaching and accepted this witness and testimony. They loved Him and rejoiced in Him 'with joy unspeakable and full of glory.'

Read your hymnbook. Do you not find that the hymns are full of this sentiment, this expression of love towards God and towards the Saviour, this desire to know Him more and more, this personal, experimental awareness and knowledge of Him? Or read Christian biographies, and you will find that this is a theme that runs right through them all. The Christian position, thank God, is not merely that I accept theoretically certain ideas about the love of God. It is something that I experience, that I know. Look at that great statement of Paul's: 'I know whom I have believed, and am persuaded that he is able to keep that which I have committed unto him against that day' (2 Tim 1:12). 'We do know,' said John in effect, 'the love that God has for us'; Christian people must know it. Do *we* know it?

I keep on repeating my question because it is to me the most vital question that we can ever face in this life and world. Let me put it like this: I do not know what the future holds for me; nobody does. Our whole life and world is uncertain, and I say that in a world like this the supreme matter is to know that God loves me—to know that I am in that relationship and that whatever happens around me, God will always be with me. Whatever may or may not come, God loves me, and I am a child of God. If I know that, then there is a sense in which anything else does not matter very much and cannot vitally and essentially affect me.

So the question remains: How may we know this—how do we know that God loves us? I will, first of all, give a general answer to the question. First, I have an increasing awareness and an increasing realisation that I owe all and everything to the Lord Jesus Christ; I am utterly dependent upon Him and the perfect work that He has done for me in His life and death and resurrection. I am bound to put that first because John puts it first. How do I know that God loves me? Is it because of some sensations or feelings? No! Rather, in the first instance, the first thing is Christ, what I feel about Christ, what Christ is to me. 'In this was manifested the love of God toward us, because that God sent his only begotten Son into the world, that we might live through him.' Do you know for certain the love of God to you? Is He central? Is He vital? Is He essential? Do you know that you are entirely dependent upon the fact that Christ is the Son of God and that He died on the cross on Calvary's hill and bore the punishment for your sins and took your guilt away? Is it all centred in Him?

If it is not, I say, go no further. If Christ is not absolutely essential and central in your position, I am not interested in what you have to tell me about your knowledge of the love of God. For the whole argument of the New Testament is that it is there that God has manifested His love, and if I do not start there, I am ignorant of what God has done. How can I love Him if I ignore that amazing manifestation and demonstration of His eternal love? That is the first test.

But let me come to the particular, and here I am simply going to give you a series of questions or statements. I agree with John that we must be particular, we must have detail. I shall suggest to you ten tests which you can apply to yourself to know for certain that you know the love of God to you.

Here is the first. It is a loss and absence of the sense that God is against us. The natural man always feels that God is against him. He would be very glad if he could wake up and read that some bishop or other had proved that God never existed; he would be ready to believe it. The newspapers give publicity to anything that denies the faith; they know the public palate. That is why the natural man is at enmity against God; he feels God is against him. That is why when anything goes wrong he says, 'Why does God allow this?' And when men and women are in a state of being antagonistic towards God, then, of course, they cannot love God. So one of the first tests, and I am starting with the lowest, is that we have lost that feeling that God is against us.

Secondly, there is a loss of the fear of God, while a sense of awe remains. Let us approach Him 'with reverence and godly fear,' writes the author of the Epistle to the Hebrews (12:28). John is going to elaborate on that; that is the rest of the fourth chapter. We lose that craven fear of God, but oh! what a reverence remains.

Thirdly, there is a feeling and a sense that God is for us and that God loves us. Now I put it like that quite deliberately because it is so very true to experience. I have lost that sense that God is against me, and I begin to have a feeling and sense that God is for me, that God is kind to me, that He is concerned about me, and that He truly loves me.

Fourthly, I have a sense of sins forgiven. I do not understand it, but I am aware of it. I know that I have sinned; 'my sin is ever before me' (Ps 51:3), as David says. I remember my sins, and yet the moment I pray, I know my sins are forgiven. I cannot understand it, I do not know how God does it, but I know He does it, and that my sins are forgiven.

A sense of sins forgiven in turn leads me to the fifth test: a sense of gratitude and thanksgiving to God. No one can believe that God sent His only begotten Son into the world to die on the cross without feeling a sense of praise and of thanksgiving. It is all pictured in the story of that man of Gadara, the man possessed with a legion of devils. No one could cure him, but Christ drove the demons out, and the man who was cured wanted to go with Jesus. 'He . . . prayed him that he might be with him' (Mark 5:18). I imagine that the man said, 'Let me be Your slave—let me carry Your bag or polish Your sandals—let me do anything I can for You—You have done so much for me.' Or think of Saul of Tarsus there on the road to Damascus. The moment he saw and understood something of what had happened to him, he said, 'Lord, what wilt thou have me to do?' (Acts 9:6). That is, what can I do to repay You—how can I show my gratitude? Do you feel a sense of gratitude? Do you want to praise God? Do you want to thank Him? When you get on your knees in prayer, is it always petitions, or do you start with thanksgiving and praise—do you feel something welling up within you? A sense of gratitude and a desire to praise is a further proof of the knowledge of God.

Then sixthly, there is an increasing hatred of sin. I sometimes think there is no better proof of a knowledge of God and knowledge of the love of God than that. You know, if you hate sin, you are like God, for God hates it and abominates it. We are told that He cannot look upon iniquity (Hab 1:13); therefore, whatever your feelings may be or may not be, if you have an increasing hatred of sin, it is because the love of God is in you—God is in you. No man hates sin apart from God.

Seventh, there is a desire to please God and to live a good life because of what He has done for us. The realisation of His love should make us not only hate sin, but also desire to live a holy, godly life. You may say your heart is cold. You are not aware of any strong emotion. But do you desire to live a better life and to please God more and more? If you are, you love God, because our Lord said, 'He that hath my commandments, and keepeth them, he it is that loveth me' (John 14:21).

Eighth, we have a desire to know Him better and to draw closer to Him. Do you want to know God better? Is it one of the greatest ambitions of your life to draw closer to Him, that your relationship to Him may be more intimate? If you have within you the faintest desire to know God better and are doing something about it, I say you love God.

Ninth, I will put this point negatively, and yet it may be the most important of all. I am referring to a conscious regret that our love to Him is so poor, along with a desire to love Him more. If you are unhappy at the thought that you do not love God as you ought to, that is a wonderful proof that you love Him. Love is never satisfied with itself; it always feels it is insufficient. The men and women who are unhappy because they do not love God more are,

KNOWING THE LOVE OF GOD

in a sense, people who ought to be very happy, because their very unhappiness at their lack of love is proof that they do love. Let me put that in the words of one of my favourite sayings, that great and wonderful and consoling sentence of Pascal's: 'Comfort yourself; you would not seek me if you had not already found me.' Love is dissatisfied, and so if I feel my heart is cold, it is a sure proof that I love Him. The unbeliever is not aware of the fact that his heart is cold, and so the negative becomes gloriously positive.

My last test is that we have a delight in hearing these things and in hearing about Him. That is one of the best tests. There are certain people in the world—alas, there are many—who find all that we have been saying utterly boring; all that we have been saying would be strange to them. Such people are spiritually dead; they know nothing about all this. So whatever the state of your emotions may be, if you can tell me quite honestly that you enjoy listening to these things and hearing about them, if you can say that there is something about them which makes things different, and that you would sooner hear these things than anything else in the whole world, then I say that you know the love that God has for you and that you love Him in return.

These, then, are some tests which seem to me to be the most practical and the most immediate that we can apply. Let me sum them up like this: Jesus Christ, the realisation of who He is, that God sent Him into the world; the realisation of what He has done by coming into the world and going back again, that He is my all and in all; the realisation that He is my Saviour and therefore my Lord, because if He has done that for me, then He has done it so that I might be rescued and redeemed out of this element of sin and that I may live a life pleasing to Him—it is all in Him. The key is my attitude towards Him. Can I say with Paul, 'That I may know him, and the power of his resurrection, and the fellowship of his sufferings, being made conformable unto his death; if by any means I might attain unto the resurrection of the dead' (Phil 3:10-11)? You need not start traveling the mystic way, you need not try to work up feelings; there is only one thing to do: face God, see yourself and your sin, and see Christ as your Saviour. If you have Him, you will have everything else. It is all in Him; without Him there is nothing.

'We have known and have believed the love that God hath to us.' Do you know that God has so loved you that He sent His only begotten Son into the world and to the cross on Calvary to die for you, to rescue you and redeem you from your sin, and to make you a child of God?

May God grant that we may be able to join in this mighty chorus on earth and in heaven which goes on saying, 'I know—yes, I know the love which God has to me'.

12
Dwelling in Love

> God is love; and he that dwelleth in love dwelleth in God, and God in him. Herein is our love made perfect, that we may have boldness in the day of judgment: because as he is, so are we in this world.
>
> 1 JOHN 4:16-17

As I have reminded you, these verses are a kind of summary of the argument which the Apostle has been developing from verse 7 of this chapter. His theme has been the importance of loving the brethren, and he is developing that argument. He has said that to love the brethren is something we should be concerned about because 'love is of God; and every one that loveth is born of God, and knoweth God.' Then he takes up this question of knowing God, and he tells us that God's great love has been manifested in what He has done for us in and through our Lord and Saviour Jesus Christ. So the great question is, do we know that? Indeed, he goes on to argue, in a subsidiary argument, that that is, in a sense, the only knowledge of God we can have. We cannot see God, but we may know Him in that vital, subjective manner, and he works out the various ways in which we arrive at that knowledge. Knowledge is very largely dependent upon objective facts— the things we have heard from the Apostles and the first Christians which we believe and accept. And having worked that out, he sums it up in the first half of verse 16: 'We have known and believed the love that God hath to us.'

Now in the second half of verse 16 and in verse 17 which we are dealing with now, we have the summing up of the other part of the argument—namely, the importance of loving one another, and the value of this in its application to our Christian experience. It is this, of course, which was John's primary object. He starts with it, and that brings him to the argument of the love of God and its manifestation. He deals with that, winds it up, and then winds up the original point with which he began; and that is what we have here.

Obviously, therefore, it is important for us to remember that these two things must always go together and be held together. We must never introduce a kind of artificial dichotomy between them; loving God and loving the brethren must always be taken together. Let me remind you again that our Lord, in His answer to the question that was put to Him when He was here on earth— 'Which is the first commandment of all?'—replied saying, 'Thou shalt love the Lord thy God with all thy heart, and with all thy soul, and with all thy mind, and with all thy strength: this is the first commandment. And the second is like, namely this, Thou shalt love thy neighbor as thyself' (Mark 12:28-31). They must always be taken together, and John shows that here, as the New Testament does everywhere in its teaching.

In other words, John here, though he has had a particular subsidiary argument, has really been summing up one great thing right through, and that is the assurance of salvation. And what he says in effect is that there is no ultimate assurance of God's love to us and of our position and our standing unless we are living the life of love. That is ultimately the ground of assurance, and that is what John wanted to leave with these people. As we have seen, when he wrote he was an old man who knew that his time on earth was coming to an end, and he wanted to administer comfort to those people. He knew about their difficulties, about the world in which they lived; he knew trials were besetting them—those insidious heresies that were raising their heads, these antichrists and false teachers, quite apart from the inherent sinfulness of society and the world. He knew all about that, and he wanted to help them; and his great argument from the beginning has been that they must be assured of certain things. There is nothing as vitally important as our certain knowledge that God has loved us in particular in Christ, and that we therefore should be able to say, 'We have known and believed the love that God hath to us.'

We can, therefore, add something to the list of ten tests which we considered earlier. You remember that we ended by saying that if we are at all uncertain about all this, if there is any hesitancy with regard to our ability to say, 'I know the love that God has to me,' if I am a little bit afraid of saying that the Son of God 'loved me and gave himself for me,' if we are unhappy about that, then the thing to do is to ask ourselves these questions. Now here we are reminded that we can add yet another, and this perhaps is still more important. The final question we therefore ask ourselves is this very practical one: Do we dwell in love? Are we living and abiding in love? That is the fourth test, you remember, which John applies: 'God is love; and he that dwelleth in love dwelleth in God, and God in him.' Not only that, but 'herein is our love made perfect'—meaning, herein is love made perfect within us—'that we may have boldness in the day of judgment: because as he is, so are we in this world.'

This, therefore, is a very vital matter for our consideration. May I put it to you in the form of two main propositions which I think are obvious and inevitable, and yet they are not only profound—they are testing, and I find them very searching. The first is that as Christians we are to dwell in love. Now what does John mean when he talks about dwelling in love? He takes that for granted about Christians. He does not stop to argue about it—he just states it. Christians are people who dwell in love; this is something vital and fundamental to them. I suggest that at the very minimum John means that Christians are those who are dwelling in an atmosphere of love, that their lives are controlled by the principles of love, that the great difference ultimately between the Christian and the non-Christian is that love is the controlling factor in the life of the Christian, whereas it is not in that of the non-Christian.

John has been elaborating this in the previous chapter,[1] where he says that the non-Christian, the worldling, is typified ultimately by Cain. That is the non-Christian position—Cain, who murdered his brother. Of course, this does not mean that every non-Christian is a murderer, but it does mean that is his mentality, his outlook; that is his spirit. He may murder with his life, as Kipling puts it, or he may murder in thought; he may murder another by the things he does to him in various ways, by things he says about him. His spirit, his outlook, his attitude is ultimately that.

The New Testament gives us many definitions of this. Paul in writing to Titus says of himself and of others before conversion that they were 'hateful, and hating one another' (Titus 3:3); that is it. But the Christian is entirely different; he is a 'new man,' and there is no respect in which he is more different than in this very matter of his spirit, of his outlook and mentality, says John. Christian men and women are characterised above everything else by this spirit of love. They abide, they dwell, they exist in a state of love—obviously so with respect to God and with respect to their fellow men and women. I have already reminded you of our Lord's answer to the question about the great commandment. In other words, as John argues and as I hope to show you, that is, in a sense, the ultimate object of salvation—to bring us into a state in which we love. That is what salvation is for, to enable us to love God and to love our neighbour as ourselves. So that is a rough-and-ready definition of what is meant by dwelling or abiding in love—love to God, love to men.

But let us become a little more particular, and John indeed forces us to do so. He has here a most extraordinary statement, the last statement in verse 17; he says, 'because as he is, so are we in this world.' Christians are people who dwell in love, and that means, says John, that they really are like God; they are like the Lord Jesus Christ. There is a great discussion amongst the authorities as to who 'he' is in the phrase 'as he is.' Some say it is God the Father; some say God the Son. I do not think we can decide which it is, but in a sense it does not matter because the Father and the Son are the same in nature, the same in character. 'He that hath seen me hath seen the Father,' said our Lord when He was here on earth (John 14:9). So we can take it as both, and the astounding and amazing statement which the Apostle makes is that we, in this world, here in this world of time, are the same as He is, there out of time and in heaven and in the eternal world. As He is in His very nature in eternity, in heaven, in glory, so are we in this world before we go to heaven; even here on earth we are like Him.

So Isaac Watts was not romancing or simply giving rein to his imagination when he talked about 'celestial fruits' growing here on earthly ground; he was stating the very thing that John is putting to us in this verse—celestial fruits, the fruit of the Spirit, which is love. That is the first thing. 'As he is'—the Father, the Son—'as he is,' and He is love; 'so are we,' even 'in this world' with all its problems and its difficulties and its trials and its contradictions. So this enables us to underline this tremendous statement a little more in detail; for us to dwell in love, therefore, means that we must have benevolence in our hearts. That is the great characteristic of God, because 'God is love.'

What, then, does this mean? Well, our Lord gave an answer in His statement in the Sermon on the Mount: 'He maketh his sun to rise on the evil and on the good, and sendeth rain on the just and the unjust' (Matt 5:45). That is God's attitude towards mankind, and 'as he is, so are we in this world.' Therefore, this attitude of benevolence towards mankind and the world at large must be in us.

But let me put it a little more particularly still. Does this not also mean that our attitude towards other people is not determined and controlled by what they are, but by the love that is in us? Now that I think needs no demonstration at all. Is that not the great characteristic of God in His dealings with mankind? God's love is not determined by us; it is in spite of us. Is that not the very essence of the whole gospel? Is that not the meaning of Christ's death upon the cross? Why did God send His Son? Was it because of something He saw in us, in any one Christian? Of course not! God's love to us is not controlled by us—not by what we do or think or say, nor by our attitude towards Him. It is something, if I may use the expression with reverence, that wells up in His eternal heart of love. There is no explanation of salvation except the love of God, caused by nothing save this self-generating love of His—not called forth by us, but emanating from Him. This, then, is the tremendous argument of the Apostle; 'as he is, so are we in this world.'

But let me go a step further and put it like this: The great characteristic of the love of God, therefore, is that God does not consider Himself—God does not consider His own honour and glory. Rather, God considers *us*. God as He looks upon us does not go on saying, 'This is what they have done to Me, this is how they have behaved with respect to Me—they have rebelled against Me; they have become offensive, ugly, and foul as the result of their attitude, and therefore . . .' Not at all! God—I say it again with reverence—in His dealings with us in Christ has not been considering Himself. He has considered us and our lost condition, and it is for that reason that He has done what He has done.

'So if we are Christians,' says John in effect, 'it means that God is in us, and God is love; therefore, we must be like that.' That means our attitude must not be determined and controlled by what other people are like or by what they do. It also does not mean that we are always to save ourselves and to claim the right of justice and honour and credit and all these other things. It means that we are not to look at ourselves and what we are doing; it means that we are to look at others and forget self in this extraordinary way and manner.

In other words, we can go a step further and put it like this: it means that, like God, we must see others as souls. We must see their need and their sorry plight; we must see them as victims of sin and of Satan. These things need no demonstration; there would not have been a single Christian were this not true of God. God looked upon us and the world, and He did not see us; He saw, rather, our captivity to Satan. He saw us in the bondage of iniquity; He saw that we were being ruined by this evil thing. He looked at us in spite of our sin; and as He is, so must we be if He is in us. 'As he is, so are we in this world'; and that means, of course that, having looked upon others, not just as they are in all their offensiveness and in all their difficulty, we see them rather as lost souls. We see them as the serfs of Satan, as the victims of these evil powers and wickednesses in the heavenly places; and we are sorry for them, and compassion enters into our heart for them.

The result is that as God is in us, so we become ready to forgive and to forget, for that is what God has done with us. God has looked upon us and forgiven us; and even more wonderful, He has forgotten our sins—He has cast our sins into the sea of His forgetfulness. What a loving, wonderful thought that is, that God not only forgives our sin, but He has forgotten all about it! Only Omnipotence can do that. Thank God He can! He does not remember my past sins; He has forgotten them, and they are gone. 'As far as the east is from the west, so far hath he removed our transgressions from us' (Ps 103:12). Blessed be His name! 'As he is, so are we'; because He is in us in this world, we must not only forgive—we must learn to forget. We must not think about our sins; we must not let them come back and dwell with us. We must banish them; we must be like God—forgiving and forgetting.

We must also become positive. We must be ready to leave our sins behind. God did not just passively decide to put our sins aside and forget them; God became active. He did something; He sent His Son, in spite of it all, into the world. Consider that great passage in Philippians 2:5-8. He did not consider Himself, He did not think of His equality with God a thing to be prized or clutched at, but He put it aside, humbled Himself, and became man. God the

Father and God the Son spoke together in the eternal council about men and women in their lost state and condition and in their need of salvation. And when the Father laid the problem before the Son and asked Him, 'Are You ready to do it?' He did not say, 'Am I to forsake heaven? Am I to humble myself? Is it fair? I am equal with You!' No! He 'thought it not robbery to be equal with God,' but that did not make Him prize and clutch at the heavenly glories. He gladly put it all on one side; He divested Himself of the insignia of His eternal glory. He humbled Himself, took upon him the form of a servant, and faced the death of the cross, never thinking of Himself.

'Let this mind be in you,' says Paul. 'Yes,' says John, 'as he is, so are we'; we are like that because He is in us. If we are truly His in this world, we are ready to come down and humble ourselves, to be misunderstood, to be laughed at and treated with scorn and derision, in a sense to be crucified—certainly in spirit, perhaps even in body—anything that may help, being always ready to do good, ready to please, not always on the defensive, not always demanding our rights and justice, but coming right down as He came down. 'As he is . . .'

You remember the argument of our Lord? He said, 'For if ye love them which love you, what reward have ye? do not even the publicans the same?' (Matt 5:46). If you do good to those who do good to you, well, what is there in it? That is the natural man, that is the animal in a sense; there is nothing special about that. This is what is special: 'Do good to them that hate you, and pray for them which spitefully use you, and persecute you' (Matt 5:44). But why should I do good to those who hate me? Here is the answer: 'Be ye therefore perfect, even as your Father which is in heaven is perfect' (Matt 5:48). John here is only paraphrasing our Lord. That is what you are to be—'perfect,' says Christ; we are to be like God who is perfect, in this respect, 'even as your Father which is in heaven is perfect.' Jesus is saying, 'Love as the Father has loved you in sending His Son into the world to die for you and to save you. "Be ye therefore perfect." As he is, so are we in this world.' That is what it means to dwell in love.

Now let me go on to emphasise the second principle. The first was that we are to dwell *in love*. Now I want to change the emphasis and say that we are to *dwell* in love; we are to abide in love. In other words, this is not to be something spasmodic in our lives and experience; it is to be the natural attitude, the place in which we dwell. You will find that word used in Scripture. For example, 'He that dwelleth in the secret place of the Most High shall abide under the shadow of the Almighty' (Ps 91:1); that is the same idea. John is particularly fond of this word 'abide.' How often have we met with it in this first epistle—abiding, continuing, going on. The man who is not a Christian does not dwell in love.

So this love is abiding; it is not spasmodic. It is not being kind to other people only when they are kind to you but *always*. God does not change. He is 'the Father of lights, with whom is no variableness, neither shadow of turning' (Jas 1:17). Thank God for that fact! What if God varied with our faults? What if He varied with us and our world, with the sun and the rain? There would never be any crops. But no; He does not change; He abides ever the same. And we are to be like that, not only when we are in the mood, not only when other people are a little bit less intractable, but always—dwelling and abiding.

How is this to be done? Does this not require perfection? Am I making the Christian life utterly impossible? Am I again to be charged with holding the standard too high? I am not complaining of such a charge; there is a sense in which I thank God if that charge is a true one. The preacher who makes the Christian life easy is one who does not know his New Testament, who is not true to his calling and commission. Here is the test: 'As he is, so are we in this world.' Christian people do not meet together to say nice things to one another. This is what we are meant to be! This is what we must be if we would have assurance of salvation and know 'the love that God hath to us.'

So I suggest that these are some of the things we have to do. We must start always by realising the doctrine, always start with truth. Love is not something that can be dealt with directly; it is always something, as it were, produced indirectly; and the way to have this love of God in us is to realise the doctrine. What I mean is this: there is only one way I know to realise the love of God, and that is to realise the truth about myself. We have to be made worse before we can be made better; there are times when we have to be cruel to be kind. We may have to clean that wound before we can put in the oil that will soothe it. We must get rid of certain things, and that is a painful process. Therefore, the highway to realising the love of God is to realise the truth about ourselves.

In other words, there is only one way to realise the love of God, and that is to realise that you are a hopeless, damned sinner, that you can do nothing about yourself. You can never put yourself right; you can never make yourself fit to stand in the presence of God. You must realise that you are altogether lost and undone and heading straight for hell, and that is where you would arrive, were it not that God in His infinite, everlasting love sent His only begotten Son not only into the world, but to the cruel death of the cross, so that you might be forgiven, that you might be saved.

Have you realised that the love of God is already in you? It is when we come to the end of self and are utterly undone and then realise what God has done for us that we begin to realise that the love of God is in us. In other words, mere abstract thoughts upon God as love will never do it. The mystics have tried that way. They have produced psychological statements. But that is not what we find in the New Testament. The way the people John wrote to experienced the love of God was in terms of sin, condemnation, and loss and what God has done about it. It is there they found love, and especially in the statements about our Lord's death upon the cross.

The second thing is meditation upon our Lord. We must recapture the lost art of meditation, and meditation especially upon Him. We must think again about that birth in Bethlehem—what it meant, what it cost, what it really involved. Try to grapple with it; it is baffling—the sacrifice, the humiliation. Look at His life; take it step by step and stage by stage. Look at what He endured and suffered through the thirty hidden years and the three busy years of his earthly ministry. Look at Him; remember what He has done and what He literally and actually suffered. Let us go over these things, let us remind ourselves of them; and then as we begin to realise what He did, we shall realise His love to us, and our love to Him will begin to develop within us and dwell with us, and also our love to others for the same reason.

Thirdly, in practice, having started with great doctrine and especially the doctrine concerning the Son of God, we have to face the situation that confronts us instead of avoiding it and turning our back upon it, excusing ourselves in terms of self-defence. I must relate every single situation that may develop in my life to the doctrines that I have been enumerating, and especially the doctrine of the cross. I am referring to that difficult person, that difficult situation in the business or office, or whatever. I do not care what it is— I repeat, I must take it and put it into the context of the cross. I must think in terms of that person; I must take the whole situation and just face it in the light of that. I must say that if God had treated me as I have treated this situation or this person, what would have happened to me? I must not avoid this; I must bring it into the open. I must flash the light of Calvary upon it, considering the heart of God which is eternal life. Is it not the case that half our troubles, and more, are simply due to the fact that we will not face the situation? We are always avoiding it. We say, 'I believe in the doctrine of the cross and God's love to me, but this situation is extremely difficult.' But we must bring these things together; the whole of my life must be controlled by this principle—the doctrine of love.

In other words, my last general word of advice would be that we must discipline ourselves. We must deal with ourselves actively, and we must deal with everything that is opposed to this life of love. This is a full-time matter. I must realise that every detail in my life counts. I am one; I cannot divide myself up into my spirit part and my other part. I cannot divide myself up into what I do on Sunday and what I do on the other six days in the week. Everything that happens to me is all a part of me. So, my whole life must be disciplined. I must watch myself and observe myself in every detail of my life, and I must mortify everything that is opposed to this love. I must discipline 'my members which are upon the earth' (Col 3:5)—my affections, lusts, passions, pride, self-glory, and all like things. I must keep them down; I must mortify them. I must deal violently with them, in order that I may become more and more like Him.

And perhaps, if I may end with one particularisation, one which is so often emphasised in the New Testament, I must watch my tongue. This 'little member,' as James called it, this unruly member, this little rudder that turns the whole ship of life, is apparently so unimportant, and yet what havoc it makes! You cannot get evil and good to come out of the same fountain; you do not get thorns and grapes from the same tree—these are the words of the New Testament (Jas 3:1-12). Control it, says the Bible. That may sound almost trivial and childish; but you know, there is a distinction between thinking and saying a thing. Do not say it, and if you do not say it you will find that you stop thinking it. Put a watch upon your lips and upon your tongue—that is one of the first things in this life of love. If you cannot control your thoughts, control your speech; and by controlling your speech you will come to use greater control upon your thoughts, and your life of love will grow and develop. This is very practical, but it is of primary and fundamental importance.

Let me give you one more general truth: The ultimate way to develop this life of love is to remind ourselves of the consequences that follow from such a development. 'Herein is our love made perfect, that we may have boldness in the day of judgment.' 'If what I have already said does not influence you,' says the Apostle in effect, 'then remember that a day will come when you will have to stand and give an account; if you want to be able to do that with boldness and with confidence, dwell in love here and now.'

13
That Great Day

> God is love; and he that dwelleth in love dwelleth in God, and God in him. Herein is our love made perfect, that we may have boldness in the day of judgment: because as he is, so are we in this world.
>
> 1 JOHN 4:16B–17

We have seen the importance of discipline, self-discipline, the importance of facing things, not excusing ourselves for our failures in avoiding the issues, and the importance of controlling what James describes as that 'little member,' that dangerous member, the rudder of a man's life in a sense—the tongue.

But we realise that was not all that could be said. John himself supplies us with other reasons and, in a sense, the profoundest reasons for giving care and attention to this matter of loving the brethren. He takes us to still higher ground and presents us here with three arguments which should always persuade us to give great diligence to this matter of loving one another.

We can summarise the three arguments in one phrase by putting it like this: We must realise the consequence of dwelling in love; and that is perhaps the most powerful argument of all. So often in our Christian lives we go astray because we do not examine the consequences of our actions. Our tendency is to live for the moment—to see things in and of themselves instead of seeing that everything belongs to everything else. Our life is not an automatic kind of life. There is danger in teaching a moment-by-moment existence in any respect, not only from the standpoint of sanctification but from any other standpoint. Our life is a continuous whole, and you cannot isolate things; everything belongs to everything else, and therefore it is true to say that as a river flowing out from its source is already destined for the sea to which it is going, so everyone born into this life is already beginning to die. The whole of our life must always be present in our minds, and we must always be doing everything in the light of its eternal consequences. Cause always produces effect, and we cannot divide these things into compartments and categories. That is the general principle which covers the three particular arguments with which the Apostle here provides us. There are three things which are inevitable consequences of dwelling in love, of abiding in love. Let us look at them.

Here is the first: To dwell in love is the final proof of the fact that God dwells in us and that we are in God. We never could dwell in love and love one another were it not for the fact that we dwell in God and God dwells in us. It is a sheer impossibility to the natural man, who is controlled by hatred and malice. The Bible is full of that teaching; it does not paint a rosy picture of human nature. I have often said, and I often feel, that if I had no other reason for believing the Bible to be the Word of God, this would be sufficient for me: the stark honesty and truthfulness of the Bible which tells the truth about man; it is the only book that does it.

We do not like this, and the world spends most of its time trying to avoid it. We praise one another; we say that if only we were given a chance, how perfect we would be! But the Bible tells us quite bluntly that we would not. The trouble is in our own heart. The truth is that we are quite incapable in and of ourselves; we cannot love as we are by nature. But the Bible shows us this grand and wondrous peace of dwelling in God and God dwelling in us. So if we do dwell in God and He in us, then obviously, and of necessity, we must be living this life of love, for 'God is love.'

Therefore, the Scripture here again causes us to examine ourselves very carefully and closely. There is no point in my saying that I dwell in love, that I dwell in God, and that God dwells in me unless I love the brethren. John works that out in greater detail when we come to the end of this particular chapter, but here is an immediate conclusion at which we arrive: If God is in me, then I must be living a life of love. Whatever I may say in terms of orthodoxy, however correct my statements may be, if I am not living a life of love, there is somewhere a lie in me. There is this artificial division between intellectual belief and assent and having the vital experience of the love of God in my soul.

Here, then, is the great conclusion which we draw. It is the last time in this epistle in which John uses this particular phrase, dwelling in God and God dwelling in us, but it is the fourth time that he has repeated it in these few verses. We have already had occasion to consider this phrase and expression, which we cannot ever understand. It is beyond us; it has eluded the great minds of all the centuries—this whole question of the mystical union between the believer and Christ—this dwelling of the believer in God and God dwelling in him. It is something that cannot be analysed and dissected; it is something you cannot put objectively in front of you and divide into its component parts. And yet it is something that is taught so constantly in the Scriptures.

There are certain, mainly negative things that we can say about this. It does not mean entering in a material sense into the life of God, nor does it mean that there is a material entry of the divine essence into me. But it does mean something like this: God in His own miraculous manner awakens in me something of His own holiness. He plants within me His holy view of life and of being and of existence. God enables me, by His operations upon me through the Holy Spirit, to understand something of His own holy nature and to view life and all its circumstances as He views them Himself.

I think this word 'dwelleth' is a most important and helpful one. 'He that dwelleth in love' means, in a sense, that God is that person's home. My home is the place in which I dwell; I spend my time there. It is where I want to be. I go about my duty, but there I dwell; my heart and mind are there. I come back as much as I can. I like to be there; I live there. They who dwell in love dwell in God. God is their home—God is where they like to be; it is with God they like to spend their time, and they arrange their lives as far as they can so that they spend a maximum amount of time there. In other words, their whole outlook upon life is God. Their thinking and meditation is thus controlled by God; it is all related to Him. They bring their minds back to God—that is what it means. Just as I take my physical body back to the home in which I dwell, so Christians, says John, take their mind and heart back to God.

Now, that is not an artificial phrase. We all know ourselves well enough to know that that is what we have to do. There are other powers and forces that would attract our minds and hearts away from God, and what we have to do is to come back—to come home to God. We are to dwell in God, and God dwells in us, which means that now the presence and the influence of God enters into our consciousness. We are aware of God; we are aware of Him permeating our life and moving and guiding us. Christians are people who dwell in love; and because they are thus dwelling in love, they are aware of the fact that God is dwelling in them. They are aware of a presence in their lives. As a person inhabits a house, so God inhabits and indwells the Christian. You are conscious of His presence and His influence and power, and you are aware of the fact that you are not living to yourself. You stand in amazement; you look at yourself, and you say, 'This is not I myself; it is God—it is God in me. What made me do that? I cannot explain it except by saying it is God who made me do it. He awakened the interest. I felt a movement, a disturbance, and God was there.'

That is what John is saying. He is saying much more than that, but that is the minimum, and what a noble and exalted statement it is concerning the Christian. If I love the brethren, if I am living this life of love, I am dwelling in God and God is dwelling in me, and my life is taken up in that way into the life of God. This is the first conclusion of dwelling in love and loving the brethren.

The second conclusion that we draw is that this is the demonstration of the fact that love has been perfected in us. That is verse 17. The Authorised Version reads, 'Herein is our love made perfect'; but it is generally agreed that the better translation is, 'Herein is love made perfect with us. Here is the perfect proof that God's love is in us.' What does that mean? It means that God's ultimate purpose in salvation and in all that He has done for us in His Son, our Lord Jesus Christ, is that we might become such people. This, says John, is the perfecting of God's love, the perfect carrying out of God's purpose of love.

Now, he has been commenting at great length about this. He says in effect, 'Herein is the love of God manifested, in that he sent His only begotten Son into the world'; and all the doctrine of the atonement came in there. Why did God do that? Why has He set Christ forth as the propitiation for our sins? Here is the answer: that is the ultimate object, the perfecting of His object and purpose—namely, that we may dwell in love, that we may love one another, that we may be in this world even as He is Himself in heaven.

This is something of which we all need to be reminded. Is there not a great danger of our thinking of salvation solely in terms of pardon and forgiveness? Is there not a great danger of our thinking of the cross and Christ's death on the cross (when we do think of them) as merely designed to enable us to be pardoned and forgiven so that we might go to heaven? But that is not the teaching of the Scriptures. That is only the first step, the grand beginning. God's ultimate object in all that He has done in His Son, the perfecting of it all, is that you and I might become like that Son; Jesus Christ is the firstborn among many brethren. He 'gave himself for us,' says Paul, 'that he might redeem us from all iniquity, and purify unto himself a peculiar people, zealous of good works' (Titus 2:14).

He has done this so that you and I might be on earth what He Himself is in heaven.

This, it seems to me, is the right way of viewing our sanctification. Sanctification must always be viewed positively and not negatively. There is nothing I know that is so tragic and unscriptural as the way in which people persist in thinking of sanctification as the mere absence of certain sins. Because they are not guilty of certain sins, they say, 'We are sanctified.' But the biblical way to test your sanctification is to ask, 'Am I like Christ?' Can I say, 'As He is, so am I in this world'? It is a positive, upward view.

In other words, the test of sanctification is our humility. If we are just thinking of sanctification as not doing certain things, then, of course, we shall be pleased, and there will be a self-satisfaction about us. But the men and women who realise that sanctification means being like Him will be those who are conscious of their unworthiness, of the darkness of their own heart. They will see themselves as falling hopelessly short; they will walk with humility because they will see so clearly the difference between the Son of God and themselves. They will be conscious of their harshness, of their bad temper, of their irritability, and of a lack of love and all these other things. And that is the object which God had ultimately in His mind when He sent His Son into the world. It is not a matter of deliverance from certain sins, but of becoming more and more like Him.

Let me sum it up in this way: Not to be concerned about loving the brethren, not to be concerned as to whether I am dwelling in love or not, is to misunderstand the whole purpose of my salvation, and therefore it is to flout God's love. If this is not the greatest concern of my life, then I am a mere beginner in the Christian life. At the beginning, of course, we have a very great concern about forgiveness; we are very concerned about certain particular sins which may have been evident in our lives before our conversion. But we must not stop at that. The hallmark of the saints is their great, increasing concern about the element of love in their lives.

They no longer think in terms of action, but in terms of their likeness to God. That is their first ambition—'as He is, so must I be in this world of time'; 'herein is love made perfect with us.' They look back to God in eternity, and they see God planning out the great way and scheme of salvation.

What is man to achieve? That is the grand objective which God had at the back of it all. He is producing a people, a special people, a people for His own possession; and they are all to be, in a sense, like Jesus Christ. There is the model, and He is fashioning and preparing us according to that model. We are not just somehow or another to get into heaven at the end, just being forgiven and no more. No! We are to develop this character, this life of Christ Himself; here and now we are to be like Him.

And that brings me to the third and last conclusion that is put here in this graphic and striking form by the Apostle: 'Herein is our love made perfect, *that we may have boldness in the day of judgment.*' Here, of course, is one of the greatest and mightiest matters that ever confronts us in the Scriptures—the doctrine of judgment, a theme which is taught in the Bible from the beginning to the very end. So what does John mean when he makes that statement? Let me put it like this: The Day of Judgment is not merely a figurative expression of what happens to us when we die. Death, of course, in a sense, is judgment, because once we die our fate is determined; but it is not death that determines our fate. Death just puts us into that place and position in which we can do nothing about it any longer. There is no second chance in the Bible. It is one thing or the other, and our destiny is decided in this life and world of time. So death is a serious matter; but it is not everything. The Day of Judgment is not death; it is rather a great event which, according to Scripture, will take place at the end of the world, at the end of time.

Now while we cannot speak too confidently or too dogmatically about the Day of Judgment, there are certain things which we can say about it. The Day of Judgment will be something formal, it will be public, and it will be final. There are those, in other words—and I put it like this in order to correct that error—who think that the Day of Judgment is just a figurative way of saying that we determine our own fate and that we will reap in eternity what we have sown in time; they say that there is no such thing as an actual Day of Judgment, with God sitting in a formal manner judging all men and the whole world. It is just a question of moral outlook, of what you have been and done. Every action has its consequence. It is just that and nothing more; it is just a way of saying that you will reap beyond death what you have been saying and doing while you are still on earth.

But that is not the Biblical teaching of the Day of Judgment. All the imagery and all the pictures that are used with respect to it in the Bible compel us to say that it is a formal event. It is a visible event, a public event, and a final event. It is something outward, something which will be seen by the whole of mankind and even by the angels themselves. It is legal; that is the picture used in the Bible for God as Judge sitting upon the throne. The books are opened, investigation is made, and sentence is promulgated. This is one of the greatest and mightiest and most extraordinary doctrines taught in the whole of Scripture—the Day of Judgment, the day of the manifestation of the righteousness and the holiness of God. A day when public sentence will be pronounced. And according to the Bible, this is a day which we are all facing and which we are all approaching. It is the teaching which you will find right through the Bible, in the Old and New Testament—and nowhere more prominently than on the lips of our blessed Lord and Saviour Himself.

What other things can we say about this? Let me give you some headings.

First of all, Christ Himself will be the Judge. In John 5:27 we read that God 'hath given him authority to execute judgment also, because he is the Son of Man.' In Matthew 25:31 we read, 'When the Son of Man shall come in his glory, and the holy angels with him, then shall he sit upon the throne of his glory,' and judgment follows. Acts 10:42 reads, 'And he commanded us to preach unto the people, and to testify that it is he which was ordained of God to be the Judge of the quick and dead.' Acts 17:31 adds, 'He hath appointed a day, in the which he will judge the world in righteousness by that man whom he hath ordained; whereof he hath given assurance unto all men, in that he hath raised him from the dead.' So the Judge who will judge all mankind at the end of time and at the end of history is none other than Jesus of Nazareth, the only begotten Son of God.

Let me ask a second question. Who is to be judged? Here the answer seems to be this: First and foremost the fallen angels, the angels who fell from their original state, are to be judged. You find this taught in the epistle of Jude and in 1 Corinthians 6 where Paul says, 'Know ye not that we shall judge angels?' (v 3). So the fallen angels are going to be judged at that great day. But it is not only a judgment of angels—it is a judgment to which every individual human being who has ever lived or ever will live will be subjected. 'We must all appear before the judgment seat of Christ'—not only the ungodly and the unbeliever, but the believer also—'that every one may receive the things done in his body, according to that he hath done, whether it be good or bad' (2 Cor 5:10). Again, Paul says in Romans 14:10, 'For we shall all stand before the judgment seat of Christ.' Revelation 20 says that God's books will be opened and that every man who has ever lived, whether believer or unbeliever, will be there confronted by the Judge.

I know, of course, that there is a difference between believers and unbelievers in this respect: There is a sense in which believers have already passed through judgment. Nevertheless, they will have to appear on the Day of Judgment. There is a difference, a distinction, and there are rewards as well as punishments; but nevertheless we shall all have to appear before His judgment seat. 'Knowing therefore,' says Paul, 'the terror of the Lord, we persuade men' (2 Cor 5:11). We will all have to appear before Him, every single human individual who has ever lived. And the time of the judgment, as I have already stated, is at the end of the world, after the resurrection of the dead.

Now I am familiar with the teaching by people who claim that there are two judgments and things of this kind. But my position is that I cannot find such things for certain in Scripture, and I am trying to say only that of which I am certain. Through the long history of the church there has been disagreement about some matters, but here there is agreement: we shall all rise, and we shall all have to appear at the judgment seat of Christ.

What is the standard of judgment? It is the revealed will of God. We are told in the Scriptures that the Gentiles will be judged according to the light they have—their conscience, says Paul in Romans 2. They will be judged according to that—the law written in their hearts, rather than the law given by Moses. But the Jews will be judged by the Old Testament revelation which they claim to be their Scriptures; they will be judged by the law given to Moses.

Christians will be judged according to the gospel they claim to believe. In other words, the Scripture teaches that there will be degrees of judgment as well as degrees of reward. Our Lord says in Luke 12 that certain people will be beaten with many stripes and some with few stripes (vv 47-48). It is a great mystery—I do not understand it; but I know what Scripture tells us. There will be differences in punishment, as well as differences in reward, according to the deeds we have done in the body.

That in its essence is the teaching of the Bible with regard to this great subject of the Day of Judgment. What John would have us see is that if we want to think of that Day of Judgment without fear, if we want to be able to face it with boldness now, and if we want to stand with boldness and not be ashamed at that great morning, we must give added diligence to loving the brethren. For if I dwell in love, then I know before I face Him on His judgment throne that I may look at Him with boldness at the Day of Judgment, because 'as he is, so are we in this world.' If I know that I have His nature in me here and now, I shall be able to face Him with boldness when I stand before Him. You see how it works: every action in my life while here on earth is important. John has already been teaching this doctrine in the second chapter of this epistle[1]. He reiterates exactly the same thing when he says, 'And now, little children, abide in him; that when he shall appear, we may have confidence, and not be ashamed before him at his coming.'

So we have looked at this third great argument, one which should surely influence each and every one of us in this matter of loving one another and dwelling in love. If I can say I dwell in love, I know that God must be dwelling in me, and I am fulfilling God's ultimate purpose in sending His Son into the world. His love is being perfected in me. And, above all, as I consider not only the nature of my life in this world but also that great day which is coming, the Day of Judgment, as I consider the revelation of God and His righteousness and the ultimate promulgation of God's sentence upon the whole of humanity, separating the good and the bad, the just and the unjust, when I think of that great day in which God will vindicate His own eternal righteousness and justice on not only the whole of humanity but on all the assembled heavenly hosts—if I want to face that without fear and without horror, if I want to face it with confidence, indeed with holy boldness, then the way to do so is to dwell in love—to cultivate this grace and to apply myself by the help of God's Holy Spirit to the perfecting of myself in love.

14
Free from Fear

> There is no fear in love; but perfect love casteth out fear: because fear hath torment. He that feareth is not made perfect in love.
>
> 1 JOHN 4:18

John here feels that this subject which he has been dealing with in the seventeenth verse is so important that he must elaborate upon it. He does not just mention it in passing; further, in the way that is always his custom, not being content with the positive statement only, he uses the negative as well. This is characteristic of all scriptural teaching, and it is perhaps the greatest proof of the profundity of that teaching and especially of its profound knowledge of us as a result of sin. We are so constituted that positives are not enough; we must have the negatives also. We need to be told what *not* to do as well as what to do. It is not enough to be given a positive picture; it must be given in contrast with the negative. Thus the Apostle says here: 'that we may have boldness in the day of judgment: because as he is, so are we in this world. There is no fear in love; but perfect love casteth out fear: because fear hath torment.'

This is concerned with punishment, and that is always something that tends to make us fearful and unhappy. 'He that feareth,' therefore, 'is not made perfect in love.' Love is not perfect in him because if it were, he would have boldness with respect to the Day of Judgment instead of being fearful and full of foreboding. John is dwelling on this ultimate consequence of our dwelling in a state of love. I suggest, therefore, that there is no better test that we can ever apply to ourselves in order to discover the quality of our Christian life and the very nature of our standing in the sight of God than to examine ourselves in the light of this great fact of the Day of Judgment.

Now John is particularly anxious to do that because it serves his ultimate object in writing his letter at all. His object is to encourage these people, to give them comfort and cheer, and to help them; and he believes in various ways and means of doing that. But in a sense, it can all be put like this: The men and women who are most happy to be in this world are those who are most happy about the next world. These things always go together; they are inseparable. So here John puts it in that particular form. The way, he says, to tell whether you are all right at the moment is to test what you feel like when you contemplate yourself at the Day of Judgment. There is, I suggest, no better test in this matter. Indeed, perhaps the supreme test of our love of God and of our love of one another is the way in which we contemplate that great day. In other words, the Apostle, having laid down his doctrine, applies it experimentally.

There again is a great principle in Scripture which we neglect at our cost: *Doctrine and application always go together*. Indeed it is possible, as we have often seen, for people to call themselves Bible students and to be very well versed in the Bible, and yet it does not profit them in the end because they never apply it. They analyse it as if they were analysing a Shakespearean play, and they are just concerned to do that; but Scripture never does that. There must always be an application. There is no value unless I test myself by it, and John does so. These things are not said for the sake of saying them; they are said with great practical interest.

The whole Biblical position, surely, is that this truth is not theoretical truth; it is not merely something to interest the mind. It is supremely interesting, but if I am only interested in it intellectually and as a system of thought, it will finally profit me nothing. This truth is given to me that I may live by it and that I may experience it in my life in all its power and grace and glory. Thank God, it is essentially practical and experimental! Therefore we must always hold these two things together, and so it comes to pass that these great statements of doctrine do become, in practice, a thoroughgoing test of our whole position. Or to put it another way, in connection with the whole subject of the assurance of salvation, there is nothing that is more important than our attitude toward the Day of Judgment.

I wonder how often we contemplate this day; I wonder how frequently we stand before it. You know, it is possible to be so interested in these various theories as to when it is going to take place that you never picture yourself standing there. It often happens that people are interested and argue about it in such a spirit as to make their whole position on that great day shaky and uncertain and unhappy. Much more important than deciding whether there are to be two resurrections, and whether the judgment goes on for a thousand years, and whether it is at the beginning or end or both—much more important than all this is the fact that you and I are facing the judgment; that is the fact that we all have to come to. Now it is that, I suggest, which John is emphasising in this eighteenth verse, and he puts it in this practical and experimental manner. And perhaps the best way we can face it together is for us to deduce some principles which seem to me to be suggested on the very surface of the statement of the Apostle.

The first is that the natural man—all of us by nature—should fear the Day of Judgment. Or let me put it like this: I say that every one of us should have known at some time or another a fear of that day. I deduce that because 'there is no fear in love,' and 'perfect love casteth out fear'; but until perfect love comes, there is fear. Indeed, it should be there, and I say *should* because I am ready to accept the fact that all do not fear. There are many people who say that they do not fear the Day of Judgment and that they never have feared it. They regard it as just a relic of primitive superstition, an aspect of biblical teaching which we ought to have shed long ago, something that is utterly inconsistent with the idea of God as a God of love. Indeed, there is a good deal of ridicule and sarcasm with regard to this Day of Judgment. There are people who are not afraid of it because they deliberately and willfully reject it with their minds and refuse to pay attention to it.

But there are others who are not afraid of the Day of Judgment because they have never thought about it; they are ignorant. The child is often not afraid of things of which it should be afraid. The child is not afraid of sitting in a motor car and attempting to drive it because it is not aware of the dangerous possibilities. Ignorance is often the great cause of a lack of fearfulness; if we are not aware of the dangerous possibilities, we will not fear them. The person who is ignorant of electricity is not as careful as the one who knows all about it. The more people know, the more they see the dangers. So there are large numbers of people in the world who do not fear the Day of Judgment because they do not think about it. They never stop to meditate; they just enjoy life as it comes along, with the latest excitement and craze. They never stop to say, 'What is the meaning of my life? What is to be my ultimate destiny?' They are not afraid of the Day of Judgment just because they have never realised that there is such a day.

But I would suggest that every thinking person knows something about this fear of the Day of Judgment.

> *The dread of something after death,*
> *The undiscovered country from whose bourn*
> *No traveller returns.*
>
> Shakespeare (*Hamlet*)

Apart from the Gospel of Jesus Christ, that is a terrifying thought. What a tremendous thing life is! We are here—we are gone. But where have we gone?

Thus conscience doth make cowards of us all.

Ibid.

There are many people in this world who do not know much about the gospel of Jesus Christ. They are not interested in it. But they are intelligent, and they have a conscience within them. There is something they want to do, and want to do very badly, and they would have done it. So why did they not do it? 'Conscience doth make cowards of us all.' Something said to them at the very moment they were about to do that thing, 'Beware! You may have to pay for this. You do not know but that there is another life.' God and all the Bible say, 'Wait a moment!.' Every intelligent man or woman knows something about this fear of the Day of Judgment. What I am speaking of, in other words, is the fear of death, what Shakespeare called our 'exit.' Shakespeare knew a great deal about this fear of God and of judgment, fear of eternity, fear of the uncertainty of it all.

I suggest that this is all quite right, and that there is nothing so superficial as the popular psychologist who tries to get rid of that, to make us like the boy whistling in the dark to persuade himself that he is afraid of nothing although he is really terrified. That is the foolish attempt of many psychologists to get rid of this fundamental thing that is so deep in the whole of human nature and which is based upon sheer intelligence. The fact is that the very thought of eternity itself surely ought to give one pause for thought and to fill one with a sense of alarm and fear, and even of terror itself, because, putting it at its very lowest, we can say that we really do not know what is coming, and men cannot prove or demonstrate scientifically that death is the end. What if it is not? Can I prove that it is? I say that is an alarming thought; there is something terrifying about the thought of that unknown 'bourn,' that unknown eternity; and I suggest that any intelligent person must of necessity know something of this fear of the Day of Judgment.

But when we get beyond the level of intelligence, there are infinitely more important reasons why we should know something about a fear of the Day of Judgment. It is not merely death, it is not merely the uncertainty of it all. Rather, we are told that 'it is appointed unto men once to die, but after this the judgment' (Heb 9:27). God, the greatness of God, the justice, holiness, and righteousness of God—we are all moving on to that. We shall all have to stand face to face with that, and the further teaching of Scripture everywhere is that my eternal destiny will there be announced—my *eternal destiny*.

I know that some do not like that and would have it explained away. Well, if you are prepared to risk all these other theories, I cannot argue with you! But the plain teaching of the Bible is that our eternal destiny is decided in this world and in this life, and that the Day of Judgment will pronounce it. I confess that I find it very difficult to understand people whose lives are not governed by this thought. There is a sense in which, if I may put it with reverence, I almost admire the courage of people who can do and say certain things—people who say harsh things about one another, people who refuse to forgive one another. I am afraid to do such things; I am afraid, because I know that I myself shall have to answer for them.

I remember once hearing of a man, and I regret to say he was a man in a very prominent position in a Christian church. There had been a quarrel between that man and certain other people in the church. The man had left that church and had been living in another town; he had been a member of another church for years, and he was now on his death-bed. The men with whom he had quarreled heard of his illness, and they met together and said, 'We admit that a great deal of the fault was on our side, and in view of the fact that he is dying, let us go and see him. It may cheer and help him.' So they took the journey, and they arrived at his house. His wife went up into the bedroom and told him they were there, but he refused to see them. I could not do that! How could I go out and face God in eternity and my whole eternal destiny and refuse to forgive a man who came to me with outstretched hand?

This is the teaching of Scripture; our Lord once put it in a parable. He spoke of a man who had sinned against his lord, and his lord told him of the punishment that was his due. But he went to his lord and said, 'Forgive me. I have nothing wherewith to pay.' 'Very well,' said the lord, 'I will forgive you everything,' and the man went out. But there was an underling who owed him something, only trivial compared with the debt he had owed his lord. This man came kneeling to him and asked his forgiveness—'I have nothing to pay you with; have mercy upon me and forgive me.' But the first man took him by the throat and said to him, 'You must pay me to the very last farthing.' Do you remember what the lord said about that man? He went back on his word of absolution, and he said, 'Bind him and cast him into prison.' 'So likewise,' says the Lord Jesus Christ, 'shall my heavenly Father do also unto you, if ye from your hearts forgive not every one his brother their trespasses' (Matt 18:35). 'Forgive us our debts,' says the Lord's Prayer, 'as we forgive our debtors.'

We do well to entertain thoughts of that unknown 'bourn'—and more so, thoughts of God and His justice, His righteousness, His holiness, and above all the love that He has manifested to us. I say once more that I cannot understand people who do not know what it is to be terrified as they contemplate the Day of Judgment. It is the most alarming, awe-inspiring thought in the universe. If you have not trembled at that thought, I beseech you, begin to think and to face it and to remember in your conversations and in your attitude and your comments about others that it is all recorded in the Book of God and may yet confront you. The way in which people can speak of one another astonishes me. I am sorry for these people who have bitterness in their hearts because I know what is happening to them and what is going to happen to them. They will spend their eternity in useless, idle remorse. The natural man should fear the judgment.

But let me come to something which is very different, thank God! This is where the gospel comes in. My second proposition is that the Christian should be free from the fear of judgment. The natural man should fear it; the Christian should be free from such fear. Is there anything that is more glorious about the gospel than just that? But there are people who dispute this. There are poor Christian people who believe that it is their duty to be miserable. There are those who say that it is presumptuous for people in this life and world, who know the darkness of their own heart and who know something of the justice and righteousness and holiness of God which I have been emphasising, to be free from that fear. In the words of Milton, they 'scorn delights and live laborious days,' afraid to say they have the joy of the Lord or the assurance of salvation.

Yet surely it is unscriptural to do so. It is the universal teaching of Scripture that we should be delivered from this fear of the Day of Judgment. Take Hebrews 2:15, where we are told that one of the main purposes of our Lord's coming and one of the main effects of His death upon the cross and of His resurrection is to deliver 'them, who through fear of death were all their lifetime subject to bondage.' It is not death but what comes after it that frightens me; but, says the writer of the Epistle to the Hebrews, that was the whole purpose of Christ's coming, that He might deliver us from this torment of death that holds us captive. Or take 2 Peter 3:12–'looking for and hasting unto the coming of the day of God.' This is the very day of which I am speaking, and this is the teaching which is to be found everywhere.

'Ye,' says the Apostle Paul in Romans, 'have not received the spirit of bondage again to fear; but ye have received the Spirit of adoption, whereby we cry, Abba Father. . . . [We] ourselves also,' he goes on to say, 'which have the first-fruits of the Spirit, even we ourselves groan within ourselves, waiting for'—that is it—'waiting for the adoption, to wit, the redemption of our body. For we are saved by hope' (Rom 8:15, 23-24). This is everywhere in Scripture, so that to assume that this is something to which the Christian is not entitled, and to consider it as a kind of presumption, is to be thoroughly unscriptural.

But the Apostle John has a particular argument to drive this point home. He says that love and fear are utterly incompatible; 'there is no fear in love; but perfect love casteth out fear.'

Now this is something that can be easily elaborated upon. Love and fear are indeed opposites; the spirit of fear is the antithesis to the true spirit of love. Think of the endless illustrations that come rushing into the mind. Think of the mother who nurses the sick child who has an infectious disease. Does she think of the possibility of catching the disease from the child? Not at all! Her love for the child casts out fear. Love and fear are incompatible, and the Apostle in this way drives home his argument.

Take, for instance, the example given by our Lord Himself when He was sending out His disciples to preach and to cast out devils. He warned them they would certainly be in danger. There would be many people who would dislike them, but this was His advice: 'Fear not them which kill the body, but are not able to kill the soul: but fear him which is able to destroy both soul and body in hell' (Matt 10:28). The way to get rid of this fear, says our Lord to these people, is, in a sense, to have this greater fear, which ultimately is the love of God; and the greater drives out the lesser.

That, then, is the first proposition, and John then goes on to say that because Christians are those in whom love has been made perfect, it follows of necessity that they should not dwell in a fearful condition; this is so because of the love of God that is in their hearts. If men and women are fearful, it means they are afraid of punishment and there is something defective in their whole conception of love. They are not loving and abiding in this state of love. So John argues that the Christian must be entirely free. Do you see the steps? Love and fear are incompatible; love drives out fear; love comes into the heart of the Christian and drives out fear; so we have no right to be fearful in this sense.

But what about the argument and the exhortation in the Epistle to the Hebrews about approaching God 'with reverence and godly fear'? What about the statement that 'our God is a consuming fire'? (Heb 12:28-29). What about the statement that 'God is light, and in him is no darkness at all' (1 John 1:5)? How do you reconcile these things? Surely the answer is provided by the quotations themselves. What John is here speaking about is a craven fear which is a very different thing from reverence and holy awe. There is, I suggest, always a sense of reverence in connection with love. You do not love a person unless you respect that person; and if men and women love God, there is a sense of awe, a holiness, about it—there is true reverence in it. 'Reverence and godly fear' is a very different thing from this 'fear [that] hath torment,' a fear that cringes and trembles. That is the thing which perfect love drives out.

So the natural man should have fear of the Day of Judgment, and the Christian should be free from that fear. How then, lastly, does the Christian become free? There are two main answers to this. The first is that Christians realise the love of God that comes to them in Jesus Christ, and the work of Christ for them. John has been elaborating on that from verse 9 in this particular chapter. To quote it once more: 'In this was manifested the love of God toward us, because that God sent his only begotten Son into the world, that we might live through him.' That is the great thing. The first way to get rid of this fear is to understand the doctrine of justification by faith only. That is why the Protestant Fathers emphasised it, and that is why only an utterly superficial idea of Christianity dislikes this doctrine. The first way for us to get rid of this fear of the Day of Judgment is to realise what God has done for us in the person and the work of our Lord and Saviour Jesus Christ.

Let me put this practically. As I contemplate myself standing before God on the Day of Judgment, I know perfectly well I am a sinner. I have offended God and have broken His law and have forgotten Him. I have not loved Him with all my heart and mind and soul and strength. I have been guilty of sins against His people and against myself. I am a sinner. How can I stand there? There is only one way in which I can stand, and that is to know and believe that He sent forth His Son to bear my sins in His own body on the tree. Hiding in Christ—nothing else can give me peace at that point. I may say that I have done a lot of good, but what is the value of good to counteract the evil I have done? There is only one thing, and it is Christ; I am hiding in Him.

> *Rock of Ages cleft for me,*
> *Let me hide myself in Thee.*
>
> Augustus Toplady

I have no other hope as I contemplate the holiness of God and the holiness of heaven. My only hope is that there is a cloak of righteousness woven by the Son of God Himself which will cover me, which will cover the darkness of my sins and my sinful life, so that I shall stand clothed and robed and perfected in my Lord and Saviour. That is the first thing to realise—the love of God and what He has done for me. Justification by faith only!

The second thing, that which John has been emphasising right through this passage, is to realise that I am a partaker of the divine nature and that God Himself has come to dwell in me, and that therefore I am like God. This is the very argument which we had at the end of the previous verse: 'because as he is, so are we in this world.' The second ground of my being able to stand with boldness is that as I contemplate the Day of Judgment I can say to myself, 'Well, as the result of applying the various tests I find in that first epistle of John, I believe that in spite of my unworthiness I am a child of God. I want to know God better; I want to love Him more. This concerns me. I do love the brethren; I like to be with them. I like reading the Scriptures. I like praying. Those are not things that are true of the natural man; so I must be a child of God. He has given me His own nature, or I would not be like that. I know something of this love of the brethren; so as I contemplate facing Him, I am a child of His! Can the Father reject His child? No! He has promised He will not do so.'

So, you see, in addition to my justification, my sanctification helps me. 'Herein is our love made perfect . . . because as he is, so are we in this world. There is no fear in love; but perfect love casteth out fear: because fear hath torment.' If we are still fearful, we are not made perfect in love; we must always take those two things together. If I do not always take justification and sanctification together, I shall be misleading myself. I shall fall into antinomianism. I shall say that if I am justified by Christ, it does not matter what I do. But John does not argue like that; it is a superficial argument. God knows I have tried it, and I know what an utter failure it is. No! Divide justification and sanctification at your peril; they are always together. Christ 'is made unto us wisdom, and righteousness, and sanctification, and redemption' (1 Cor 1:30).

What is the relationship of these two? It is most important and interesting. I put it like this to you: There is the immediate and the mediate way of getting rid of the fear of the Day of Judgment; or if you prefer, there is a direct and an indirect way, and you need both. The immediate or the direct way is to understand the doctrine of justification by faith only. When I feel utterly condemned and hopeless and sinful, there is only one thing to do: I can rely upon nothing but the work of Christ for me. I cannot rely upon my acts; they are the cause of my misery. 'Therefore being justified by faith, we have peace with God . . .' (Rom 5:1). Thank God for that! So if you find yourself on your death-bed with the memory of an old sin, or if you have done something or thought something you know to be wrong and you do not have time to start living a better life, I say, just hide yourself in Christ; you are all right—you are justified by faith only.

But do remember the other side—the indirect or the mediate method, which works like this: If I am not living the Christian life, and love is not perfected in me, I will have a constant sense of condemnation and of fearfulness. I will spend the whole of my life in this world in condemnation. My whole life will be lived in misery, and I am not meant for that. I am meant to live a life of joy and of peace and happiness; I am meant to have boldness as I contemplate the Day of Judgment.

So how do I do that? Here is the answer: Live a life of love; let love be perfected in you. Love the brethren, and as you do so you will say to yourself, 'In spite of what I am, I find that as He is, so am I in this world.' You will find yourself loving someone who is hateful, and you will draw the correct deduction and will say, 'It must be that Christ is in me.' You will come to the Day of Judgment without fear or trembling. So sanctification indirectly, mediately, will act with the justification that does it directly and immediately, and that is the prescription that is prescribed by the Apostle at this particular point.

Let us be clear as to the position here. We will not be perfect in this world, but as we dwell in Christ and as we manifest this love, we will know that we are in God and God in us. We will realise that we have nothing but Him; that though we are still imperfect, 'He which hath begun a good work in [us] will perform it until the day of Jesus Christ' (Phil 1:6). He will perfect us, and so at the end He will 'present [us] faultless before the presence of his glory with exceeding joy' (Jude 24). The more I am like Christ, the less I will fear the Day of Judgment, and the greater will be my boldness as I think of it and as I contemplate it.

May God give us grace to bear in mind and apply these three steps: The natural man should fear the Day of Judgment; the Christian should not fear the Day of Judgment; and Christians should not fear it because they are justified by Christ and sanctified by Christ and made like Christ and will ultimately be with Christ.

15
Members of the Same Family

We love him, because he first loved us. If a man say, I love God, and hateth his brother, he is a liar: for he that loveth not his brother whom he hath seen, how can he love God whom he hath not seen? And this commandment have we from him, That he who loveth God love his brother also. Whosoever believeth that Jesus is the Christ is born of God: and every one that loveth him that begat loveth him also that is begotten of him.

1 JOHN 4:19–21; 5:1

I take these four verses together because it seems to me that in them the Apostle sums up, and therefore brings to a conclusion, everything that he has been saying upon this vital and important theme of loving the brethren, which he began to treat in detail in the seventh verse of this fourth chapter. Fortunately for us, he does so in terms of four propositions, and each one of them is to be found in each of the four verses. But before I touch upon them in detail, I would remind you again that the Apostle's argument is that really this is a matter which needs no demonstration; it is something that ought to be quite inevitable to us, and unless we realise that this is something inevitable in the Christian life, our understanding of the whole position is, to put it at its lowest, seriously defective. Wise man and able pastor as he was, John realised that it was not enough just to say that. He knew that we need to be reminded of the particular argument, and here, therefore, he proceeds to work out these arguments with us in detail.

I shall summarise them here because there is a sense in which we have already worked them out in detail, even as John himself has done. The argument is the one we find in verse 19, which reads in the Authorised Version, 'We love him, because he first loved us'; or perhaps it is better expressed in the Revised Version: 'We love because he first loved us.'

Now that is one of those great and glorious statements in which, again, you have an account and summary of the whole gospel. John has already been saying this in different ways. He said in verse 10, 'Herein is love, not that we loved God, but that he loved us, and sent his Son to be the propitiation for our sins.' We are incapable of love apart from what God does to us. So he concludes that we love because God first loved us. Now there he is saying something like this: Everything, of course, is of God; there would be no such thing as Christianity at all were it not for the love of God. God's love is entirely unmoved by anything in us—by any merit or worthiness in us, or by anything that God has ever seen in us. We must once and for ever get rid of the idea that God has loved us by way of a response either to something that is in us or to something we have done. 'When we were enemies, we were reconciled to God by the death of his Son' (Rom 5:10).

The scriptural teaching is that man is in sin; he is dead and vile, and there is nothing in him to call forth the love of God. Rather, God Himself has been moved by nothing but His own everlasting love. We love because He first loved us. The love of God is self-generated, self-moved, self-created; and it is the very first postulate of the Christian gospel to realise that. But the statement really does not stop at that, because John was concerned about this practical object that he had in mind. So what he is really emphasising is not only that God has loved us in spite of ourselves, but that the effect of God's doing so has been to create love in us. The outcome, as it were, of God loving us is that we should also love God and love one another.

Now here again is something we have seen several times as we have been considering this elaborate statement. 'Herein,' says John, 'is our love made perfect.' In other words, that is the objective of God's love. God has not merely loved us in order that we might be forgiven and saved from hell and thus be rescued from the punishment of sin. God's whole work in us was designed to produce a certain type of person. He has set out to produce a new race, a new generation, and we are all to be modeled on the pattern of our Lord Jesus Christ. He is 'the firstborn among many brethren' (Rom 8:29); we have been 'created in Christ Jesus unto good works, which God hath before ordained that we should walk in them' (Eph 2:10).

So Christians are to be like our Lord Jesus Christ and to reproduce the love of Christ in their lives. Read the Gospels about Him, and you find that He had an eye of compassion; He saw need and suffering. He did not deal with people according to their deserts, but according to His own love. His attitude toward people was not determined by what they were, but by His love to them. And that, says John, is the kind of love that is to be in us; we love, because He first loved us. Thus the inevitable corollary or conclusion which we must draw from realising that God has loved us is that we are to be creatures also who love; and we are to love in the same way as the Lord Jesus Christ Himself loved when He was here on earth, and as He still loves us from His throne in heaven.

Now that is the Apostle's first argument, of which we must never lose sight. An ultimate test, in other words, of our profession of the Christian faith is whether we have within us this quality of love. You cannot read the New Testament without seeing this. It is not our good works or our merit that matters. It is not our zeal, even as preachers of the gospel; we may do that with carnal zeal and with a hard heart. No; the ultimate test is love. It is not something theoretical, nor is it something to which we subscribe on paper. The ultimate test of our conformity to the Lord Jesus Christ is that we manifest this love in our lives and in the whole of our conduct.

The second argument, found in the twentieth verse, is perhaps a little more difficult: 'If a man say, I love God, and hateth his brother, he is a liar: for he that loveth not his brother whom he hath seen, how can he love God whom he hath not seen?' Now the first argument was from the very nature of the gospel, but I would describe this one as an argument from common sense. Here is a man who says, 'I love God,' but it is obvious in practice that he hates his brother. He does not speak to his brother, or he is annoyed with him; he will have nothing to do with him. So his whole attitude towards his brother is one of hatred rather than of love. Well, says John, the only thing to say about that man is that he is a liar. This Apostle is fond of that term. He uses strong language, and he does not apologise for doing so. Such a man is 'a liar'; he does not love God—that is obvious: 'he that loveth not his brother whom he hath seen, how can he love God whom he hath not seen?' The thing is a sheer impossibility.

Now there are two difficulties that present themselves to people as they consider this verse. The first is that we tend to think instinctively that it is easier to love God than to love our brethren, and we think so for this reason: The brother is guilty of sin; he is not perfect, and there are many things about him which we dislike. But as for God, God is perfect; God is without sin. He has no flaws, nothing which is in any way objectionable in His character or in His nature. Therefore, we tend to argue, in human terms only, that it ought surely to be easier for us to love God than it is to love our brother. There are so many hindrances and obstacles to loving our brother which are entirely absent in the case of God. Therefore, we feel at first that John's argument is put the wrong way round and that it is not easier to love the brother whom we have seen than the

God whom we have not seen. So it comes to pass that we often delude ourselves into thinking that while we do not love our brother, we really do love and are concerned about our love to God.

The second objection is a more biblical and perhaps a more theoretical one. There are those who feel that this statement here is a contradiction of what we find our Lord saying in the Gospels with regard to the question of the great commandment: 'Thou shalt love the Lord thy God with all thy heart, and with all thy soul, and with all thy mind. This is the first and great commandment,' He said. 'And the second is like unto it, Thou shalt love they neighbor as thyself' (Matt 22:37-39). There the order seems to be, love God first and then love our neighbor. But John seems to reverse the order, some people argue; he says that you must start by loving your brother, and as the result of so doing, you come to love God. People thus feel that John here seems to be supporting an argument which has been so common in this century. It is that of the man who says, 'I don't know much about loving God, but I do know about loving my fellow-man, and if a man loves his fellow-man he must love God.'

These are the difficulties, and we can answer them like this: John does not teach here that we must start by loving our fellow-men and women and then advance from that to loving God; that is an entirely false deduction from this statement. John is not saying, 'If you only love your fellow-man first of all because you see him, that will help you to rise up to the level of God, and you will begin to love Him.' Not at all! Rather, John says that if a man says he loves God and does not love his brother, he must be a liar. Or perhaps we can best explain it by saying that there is no separation between what our Lord called the first and second commandments. Our Lord indeed coupled the two together, and that must be so for this good reason: If the first commandment is that I should love the Lord my God with all my heart and mind and soul and strength, then it must follow of necessity that I am greatly concerned about doing what God asks me to do. And what does God ask me to do? The first thing He asks is that I should love my brother.

So there is a sense in which I cannot love God without loving my fellow-man at the same time; to love God is, of necessity, to love those who are loved by God. Intellectually, of course, we draw distinctions between loving God and loving the brethren, but in actual practise, because of the nature of love and because of the nature of our love to God, it is impossible to love God and to desire to please Him without loving the brethren, because that is what God desires from us.

Thus it seems to me we can put it like this: John here is really getting down to our level and being essentially practical. John is, I imagine, countering some of the heresies and the false teachings that were current in his time, even as they are today. One of the greatest dangers that always confronts us is the danger of what I must again describe as a false kind of mysticism. There is nothing easier in this Christian life than for us to devote our time and attention to the cultivation of our soul. We begin to read manuals on the devout life, and they all exhort us to this pure love of God. They all tend to make us think that it is a matter of feeling and sentiment. We can be outwardly seeking to develop the love of God in our own heart, and yet the whole time in our actual practise, conduct, and behaviour we may be irritable, bad-tempered, and selfish. And what John is concerned to do is to correct that particular danger and tendency.

So he puts it, therefore, in this practical form. He is out to show that to love God is always something practical; he is going to tell us in the next verse that to love God means to keep His commandments. Our Lord elaborated that theme time and time again. He said, 'He that hath my commandments, and keepeth them, he it is that loveth me' (John 14:21). He is not the man who gets himself into ecstasies when he is alone, nor is he someone who is conscious of wonderful feelings. He is the person who keeps our Lord's commandments. If we do not keep them, we are not truly loving God, for the way in which love manifests itself is by keeping the commandments.

This is surely something that is obvious. Is it not evident in our ordinary human relationships? That is where some of the poets are often misleading. They could often say beautiful things about love, but they did not always practise it. Sometimes they were the most difficult men imaginable. It is hard to understand, but the explanation is that love to them was just a sentiment. They were difficult men to live with; their own personal life was often a tragedy, including their married life, because they were unable to see that love is something essentially practical. You really show your love to a person not by just writing letters or thinking beautiful thoughts, but by being practical and doing things which help that person and by showing love in actual conduct and behaviour.

That is the essence, I think, of the argument on this point. Indeed, I can go further. Because we are what we are, actual sight is a great aid to our love. If, of course, we were perfect, then it might be as easy to love someone whom we do not see as it is to love someone whom we do see. But in our state of imperfection and with sin still clinging to us in this world and life, it is the simple truth to say that sight is a great aid and help to our love.

But I can imagine someone objecting at this point and saying, 'But isn't it true that absence makes the heart grow fonder? How do you explain that in the light of what you have just been enunciating?' My reply to that would be that it is perfectly right in certain senses to say that, but it is a statement that always must be qualified. Because we are what we are, if that absence is prolonged, far from making the heart grow fonder, it may bring an end to love. Is it not true to say of all of us that we tend to forget, and if a certain object is removed out of our sight, then unfortunately, even at our best and at our highest, we may forget that object or person?

For instance, do you see that person suddenly bereft of another, breaking his or her heart, and you say, 'How is that poor person going to live?' It seems to be impossible, but you see that person in five or ten years time and the position seems to be very different. There is a calmness and composure and an almost jovial happiness about them. How do you explain it? 'Well,' you say, 'time is a great healer'; and that is what balances the saying that 'absence makes the heart grow fonder.' It did not make the heart fonder, because the absence was prolonged; the person, being frail and fallible, forgot the other person, and thus the anguish has been removed. Therefore, we must be very careful of these attempts of ours to philosophise concerning life. The fact is, and I think we see how essentially right John is in his argument, because we are what we are, sight and vision and contact are of great help, and that is why John argues as he does.

Let me put it quite directly and bluntly like this: The most difficult thing for each one of us is to love God. How we fool ourselves in much of our talk about loving Him. 'No man hath seen God at any time,' as John has reminded us, and it is because we cannot see Him with the naked eye that it is so difficult to love Him. It is a help to be able to see the object that calls forth our love; we know this from our own human experience. Faith, hope, love—and the greatest of these is love; it is the last thing at which we arrive. We feel a sense of gratitude to God, a sense of dependence upon Him long before we really love Him. To love God is the highest achievement of the Christian in this world and in this life. Therefore, John's argument is perfectly right: It is easier to love the brethren whom we have seen than it is to love God whom we have not seen.

Thus the next step in the argument is that what we see in the brother is nothing but the love of God, and therefore John's conclusions must be right. If we are not doing the easier, how can we do the more difficult? This is not a matter of argument, says John. The only thing to say about the people who say they love God and hate their brother is that they are liars. They are persuading themselves that they are loving God when they are not loving Him at all. For if they know anything about the love of God, they know that those who hate their brother cannot be loving God, because

God has loved them even though they were sinners. To know anything about the love of God is to know it means loving the unworthy, loving that which is objectionable.

They know that is the end from which they start; that is the whole basis of their position. And therefore if they do not love that brother whom God has loved in spite of himself, they know nothing at all about love. Christians look at this brother, and as they see him they say, 'Yes, there is a man who like myself has been dealt with by God in His love and grace and compassion. I must learn to look at him as God looks at him and as God looks at me.' The state of the brother should, therefore, stimulate these thoughts of love; and thus by loving the brother whom they have seen, they love the God whom they have not seen. The love of God and the love of our neighbour are indissoluble and indivisible.

There, it seems to me, is that second argument which so often has caused people to stumble because of its apparent contradiction of certain things which we have always believed and certain teachings on the Scripture. It is easier to love the brother whom we have seen than it is to love God whom we have not seen. And here we see the great condescension of God. He does not ask us to face that impossible task of loving Him in that manner. He has told us that the way for us to love Him is to love these brethren who are His. If we love them, we are loving Him, because it is His love shed abroad in our hearts that enables us to do it.

Then John goes on to the third argument, which we find in the twenty-first verse where he says, 'And this commandment have we from him, That he who loveth God love his brother also.' Now the connection can be put like this: 'I have been talking about loving God and about loving one's neighbour,' says John, 'and I have been saying how these things inevitably go together. That reminds me of the actual commandment which God gave us, so that there is no reason whatever for arguing about these matters. If I say I draw these deductions from the nature of the gospel and the nature of the love of God, I am confronted by that commandment, and whether I like it or not, that is God's commandment.'

God has commanded this from the beginning. You find it with Cain who hated his brother Abel, and Cain was dealt with by God. You find it plainly taught in the commandments that God gave to the children of Israel through Moses. Love to God, love of our neighbour—it is put both negatively and positively, so that we are not left in the realm of merely drawing our own conclusions and deductions. God commands us to love one another.

'But surely,' says someone, 'isn't it rather ridiculous to command anyone to love? You cannot command your moods and affections.' There again we are dropping into the error of misunderstanding the true nature of love. What he means by commanding us to love is that I am not governed by my immediate instincts. I do not just obey impulses that come to me; rather, as a Christian I have a new view of life, a new outlook. I do not look at men and women and see them as they are; I see them all in the light and teaching of God's Word. And the moment I begin to think about them like that, my very attitude towards them is changed, because I realise now that I have to look at them with the eye of God, and thus it is essentially right that we should be commanded to love.

This does not mean that I work up feelings; but, as we have already seen, it does mean that whatever my feelings may be with respect to that brother, I must treat him as a brother. I must act towards him as if he were a lovable character; I must do to him what God has done to me. I must not see the sin, but I must see the heart and soul behind it. I must have compassion upon him, and if I deal with him in that way, such is the alchemy of God's love that I shall face even my feelings with respect to him as a challenge, and I shall begin to experience even the sentiments towards him which I have hitherto regarded as the expression of love. So God commands us to love the brethren, and we do so in that particular way and manner.

And that brings me to the last argument, which is the statement of the first verse of the fifth chapter: 'Whosoever believeth that Jesus is the Christ is born of God; and every one that loveth him that begat loveth him also that is begotten of him.'

'True Christians,' says John in effect, and he is emphasising what he has said many times already, 'are people who have been made partakers of the divine nature. They have been born again; they have been born of God. They have not just decided to become Christians and to do certain things. No; God has worked in their souls, and therefore the Holy Spirit has produced a new nature, a new man, in them, and that new nature is nothing but the nature of God Himself. They are people who have been begotten by God.

'That,' says John, 'is the position and the truth of an individual Christian. But it is also true of that other Christian. These two people are now children of God, and therefore they are brothers. They are members of the same family; they have been begotten by the same Father; they are sharing the same nature; they have the same interests and outlook, the same blessed hope, the same everything.

'Now,' says John, 'this does not need any argument. It follows quite simply and naturally that to love the Father must of necessity mean to love the brethren. It is not unnatural, is it, even on the human plane for members of the same family to love one another? We are more ready to forgive things in those who are related to us than we are in people who are not. I am speaking of the natural man who is very lenient to the faults and failings of his own family, his own children, or parents, or his own brothers or sisters. That is nature; it may be selfish, but it is true to nature; and members of the family, those who share the same blood, love one another.

'Well, that is the principle that operates in the spiritual realm,' says John, 'and as it is unnatural for brothers not to love one another, so it is equally unnatural for those who claim that they are partakers of the divine nature and sharers of God's own nature not to love one another. If you really are in the Christian position,' says John, 'you are members of this self-same great family.'

So you work out the Apostle's argument like this: Consider

that other person, that other brother in the church whom you find objectionable in so many respects. I do not hesitate to repeat that, because as I have emphasised several times, we are not told to *like* but to *love* one another. There are certain things about people that we do not like, but we love them in spite of that. So we look at these other people and remind ourselves that they are children of God and are heirs of heaven and eternal bliss, even as we are ourselves. We say, 'Those people are going to be in heaven as certainly as I myself am going to be there. I shall have to spend eternity with them. Is it common sense, therefore, that I should be acting the way I am towards them? I shall not be able to turn away from them in heaven. Everything is open in heaven; everything is light and there is no darkness.'

So I begin to argue like that, and I begin to take myself in hand, and I see that I am absolutely wrong not to love them. I am permitting something in my heart that is a negation of everything I am looking forward to. I then ridicule such an attitude; I see it as a barb of Satan. I draw it out and get rid of it, and, in spite of the things I still dislike, I love the brother. My relationship to him makes me do that; my realisation of the fact that this man and I are heirs of God and joint-heirs with Christ makes me face this essential contradiction. The moment I do this, my difficulty vanishes, and above everything else, I find that my communion with God is again restored, and I enjoy this full fellowship with Him and that abounding joy about which the Apostle is so concerned.

That, therefore, it seems to me, is the essence of the argument that John has developed with regard to this vital and important subject of loving the brethren. Shall I put it in a final statement in this form? Are you enjoying fellowship with God? Do you know that God is your Father? Are you enjoying communion with God? When you get on your knees to pray, do you know God is there? Have you found Him? Do you feel that God is near you when you need Him? Have you confidence when you pray? Are you aware of receiving power from the Lord Jesus Christ to overcome your difficulties?

That is what you are meant to have; that is why John writes his letter: 'that ye also may have fellowship with us: and truly our fellowship is with the Father, and with His Son Jesus Christ' (1:3). 'I want you to enjoy it also,' says John in effect, 'and you can enjoy it.' So, are we enjoying it? If we are not, is this, I wonder, because we are not loving the brethren? Fellowship with God is an utter impossibility if we are not loving the brethren; it is impossible, it cannot happen.

Therefore, if we are not enjoying these full benefits of the Christian life and experience, that is surely the first subject for self-examination. Start with the brother whom you do see; start with the person who is right in front of you. Put yourself right on that, and if you feel you cannot, ask God to help you; confess with shame your failure and sin. Tell him about the hatred that is in your heart, expose it to yourself, and ask God to help you to get rid of it, to take it out of you, and to fill and flood you with His own love. Go to God about it, and keep on going until you have conquered and got rid of it; and the moment you find you are loving your brother, I assure you, in the name and the character of God, that you will find your fellowship and communion with God restored; you will be basking in the sunshine of His face, and your whole life will be flooded with His divine love.

Oh, this is a practical matter! Love is not a sentiment; it ultimately means being in this relationship to God. May God give us grace to be honest with ourselves, to examine and to search ourselves, to not allow the devil to make us delude and fool ourselves— 'If a man say, I love God, and hate his brother, he is a liar.' Let us, rather, humbly before God examine ourselves and thus rid ourselves of these hindrances to the full experience of the communion and the fellowship of God and the joy of His salvation.